PUBLIC LEADERSHIP INSTITUTE

Voicing Our VALUES

A message guide for policymakers and advocates

FOURTH EDITION

BERNIE HORN AND GLORIA TOTTEN

Public Leadership Institute
1823 Jefferson Place NW, Washington, D.C. 20036
www.publicleadershipinstitute.org
Tel: (202) 454-6200

Printed in the United States

Public Leadership Institute books are manufactured by environmentally responsible processes, including the use of acid-free recycled paper.

Library of Congress Cataloging-in-Publication Data
Horn, Bernie, 1956-
Voicing Our Values: A message guide for policymakers and advocates / Bernie Horn and Gloria Totten
p. cm.
ISBN 978-0-9991024-2-8 (paperback)
1. Communications in politics—United States.
2. Progressivism (United States politics)
3. Politics, Practical—United States. I. Title.
JK2316.H67 2019
324.2736—dc22

Fourth Edition

TABLE OF CONTENTS

INTRODUCTION

HOW (AND WHY) TO USE THIS BOOK

HOW (AND WHY) TO USE THIS BOOK

Politics is the art of persuasion. But persuasion is hard and getting harder. Today, facts are rationalized away and lies are ubiquitous. Without a grasp on objective truths, how can we get Americans to even comprehend what's in their self-interest, much less what's best for our nation?

It's a challenge. As you will see, facts and logical arguments, by themselves, are not particularly persuasive. You need to be aware of your listeners' preconceptions and biases, start from a point of agreement, articulate your progressive values, and show listeners how they benefit—all while using language that nonpolitical Americans are willing to hear.

It's important to note that, while much of the guidance provided in this book is to help you with your interpersonal communication with constituents and colleagues, through one-on-one or via speeches, it can also help inform your mass communications, such as emails, newsletters, constituent letters, websites, etc. Simply take some time to think about who you are communicating to—what do you know about them, what have they written in their email or letter to you, what problem are they trying to get you to address? Then, the same rules apply: 1) start from a position of agreement ("I agree that..."); 2) articulate your progressive values (I believe that..."); and 3) show them how they will benefit (I hope you know that I am trying to...for you and your community").

In every case, you must communicate, over and over again, in words they understand, that you are on their side.

Throughout this volume, we offer suggested language to demonstrate what progressives should and shouldn't say. We hope it makes this volume easy to use. As long as you understand the reasoning behind our recommendations, we encourage you to adapt the examples to your own voice.

Make the language authentically yours, fully integrating it with your own knowledge and experience. Similarly, when given the opportunity, tell a story that helps your listeners picture the problems you seek to address and the goals you seek to achieve.

Messaging is not a silver bullet. In politics, it's just one tool of many. But if we combine better messaging with problem-solving policies and bold advocacy, we can mobilize the majority of Americans who agree with us, win our electoral and policy campaigns, and change the world.

SECTION ONE

HOW TO PERSUADE

HOW TO PERSUADE

1. The Science of Persuasion

For most of the 20th century, political science, economics and philosophy relied on the premise that people base their opinions and choices on facts and logical reasoning. More recently though, thousands of studies have proven that people actually rely on emotion and ingrained beliefs far more than they employ objective facts or logic.

In his book *Thinking Fast and Slow,* Nobel Prize-winning scientist Daniel Kahneman summarized this field of research, describing dozens of ways that cognitive biases skew human reasoning. Many other scientific books and articles confirm that human minds are predisposed to believe falsehoods and exaggerations because of biases, heuristics and fallacies. But there is one cognitive bias that is particularly important to understand if we are to be successful in politics.

Confirmation bias

It is confirmation bias. This is when people seek out information that conforms to what they already believe or want to believe, while—inside their minds—ignore or refute information that disproves those assumptions.[1] It is a selective use of evidence through which people reinforce to themselves whatever they want to believe.

Confirmation bias is one of the oldest-known and best-proven cognitive biases. Sir Francis Bacon explained it 400 years ago. In the 21st century, it is accepted science.

If people believe that violent crime keeps increasing, they will retain infor-

1 We use this term generically, as others do, to encompass associated labels which describe how people irrationally confirm and defend their beliefs and desires, such as *motivated reasoning, desirability bias*, and *disconfirmation bias*.

mation about recent crimes and disbelieve or ignore the fact that crime rates have declined for decades. If individuals think the Earth is thousands, instead of billions, of years old, they will not believe the truth even when shown fossils in a museum. For that matter, if people are convinced that Friday the 13th is unlucky, they will pay attention and remember the times bad things happened on this date but will fail to remember all the Friday the 13ths when no misfortune occurred.

In short, when faced with facts that contradict strongly felt beliefs, people will almost always reject the facts and hold on to their beliefs.

Confirmation bias is crucial because, when it comes to politics, all of us carry in our heads a long list of preexisting beliefs, stereotypes and biases. So, if you present evidence or use language that seems to challenge your listeners' key beliefs, they will stop listening. If they think you are saying "you're wrong," a switch clicks in their brains turning off rational consideration and turning on negative emotions.

Why do people's brains work that way?

Bias inside the brain

Psychologists widely use the labels System 1 and System 2 to describe two main memory systems in the human brain. System 1 is the "fast" system which reacts instantaneously, reflexively and emotionally. This part of the brain is automatic, intuitive and subconscious. System 2 is the "slow" system that is deliberate, controls abstract thinking, and stores memories such as facts and events. The System 2 part of the brain is more rational and reflective.

Because System 1 operates in milliseconds, its reactions can override or redirect System 2's slower reasoning. If your listener's reflexive system determines that you are attacking an important belief, it will divert thinking away from the rational mechanisms in the brain to emotional ones. Simultaneously, the listener's mind will cherry-pick memories to reinforce the preexisting belief that seems to be under attack. In other words, System 1 will engage the "fight or flight" reflexes that protected the evolving *homo sapiens* in order to protect our modern-day beliefs.

Let us imagine you are discussing voter fraud with an irascible neighbor who believes it's a problem and you say, "There is no evidence of massive voter fraud," which is unquestionably true. His brain will perceive your words as an attack, he will feel a strongly negative emotional reaction, he will then remember and focus on the very real-to-him fake news that sup-

ports his belief in voter fraud, and you will have no chance to persuade him of anything. Your effort at persuasion has failed.

As political activists, we wish that we could reason with people and have calm, cool, dispassionate discussions about public policy. But instead, we tend to trigger in our listeners a negative emotional response, reminding them of memories that reinforce those negative emotions. We are arguing with ghosts from our listeners' pasts—and losing.

Clinical psychologist Drew Westen of Emory University used functional magnetic resonance imaging (fMRI) to examine what was going on in the brains of partisans who supported either George W. Bush or John Kerry during the 2004 presidential contest. He gave test subjects a series of openly contradictory statements from each candidate. Based on confirmation bias, he expected that each partisan would overlook the contradictions of his or her own candidate while indignantly protesting the contradictions of the other guy. And just as Westen (and Sir Francis Bacon) would have expected, the test subjects did precisely that.

When Drew Westen looked at the fMRIs, the subjects—not too surprisingly—had not engaged the logical parts of their brains. They had engaged their emotions instead. And then, after rationalizing away legitimate attacks on their favored candidates, the brain's pleasure center released the neurotransmitter dopamine. As Westen explained in his book *The Political Brain:*

> Once partisans had found a way to reason to false conclusions, not only did neural circuits involved in negative emotions turn off, but circuits involved in positive emotions turned on. The partisan brain didn't seem satisfied in just feeling better. It worked overtime to feel good, activating reward circuits that give partisans a jolt of positive reinforcement for their biased reasoning. These reward circuits overlap substantially with those activated when drug addicts get their "fix," giving new meaning to the term political junkie.

Election lie ...

This means that when you attack preexisting beliefs, not only are your arguments rejected, but you are also helping to emotionally reward partisans for their stubbornness, deepening their attachment to false ideas.

The leaders of the radical right seem to understand all of this. They know that conservative voters are not searching for truth. They are, instead, consciously or unconsciously, seeking out information that conforms to their preexisting beliefs. That's why those voters watch Fox News, listen to Rush Limbaugh, and read Breitbart. That's also why conservatives are so susceptible to “fake news” on the Internet. They believe the lies because they want to—it quite literally feels bad to admit one is wrong and feels good to assert one is right.

In sum, there are tremendous barriers in the path of persuasion. How do we work around those obstacles?

2. Three Rules of Persuasion

Avid partisans are invested in their preexisting beliefs, so they're very hard to persuade. There are conservatives, for example, who remain immovable no matter how many scientists testify to the truth of climate change, no matter how much evidence shows that the death penalty doesn't deter murder, no matter the incontestability that voter fraud is too rare to be concerned about.

These conservatives are completely locked into their confirmation bias. They will even alter or forget previous core beliefs (e.g., for personal morality, against deficits, opposed to Russia) in order to hold on tightly to current ones. Facts are completely overrun by their emotions.

But among less-partisan *persuadable* Americans, confirmation bias can be overcome. These swing voters don't lack political beliefs, biases and stereotypes. Rather, they carry in their minds both progressive and conservative ideas and can be persuaded by either. In addition, because they don't hold onto those beliefs with the intensity of partisans, they don't feel as much emotional need to defend them.

That presents us with a golden opportunity for persuasion, if only policymakers, advocates and activists understand these Americans: They're not like us.

Progressive activists know a great deal about issues, and we tend to pick our favored candidates based on the policies they trumpet. When progressives talk to each other about politics, we assume our listeners know (and care) quite a lot.

Persuadables, in contrast, don't pay much attention to public policy. They don't often read or watch the political news. As a result, they are the citizens who tend to know the least about issues, legislation and the political process. And as polls have consistently shown, they care the least too.

Therefore, progressives' other problem in persuasion is that we tend to talk to swing voters the same way we talk to each other. We assume these voters know what we know, think the way we think, and are persuaded by the facts and arguments that persuade us. That simply doesn't work.

If you are to persuade undecided Americans, the most important thing to understand is that when they are considering political candidates and causes, there is one overriding (but vague) question in their minds: "Who is on my side?" That is the fundamental element of persuasion. And since you cannot change people's beliefs, you must use *beliefs already in their minds* to persuade them that you are *on their side*.

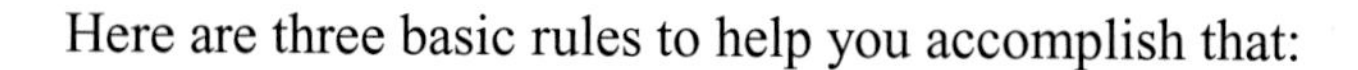

Here are three basic rules to help you accomplish that:

First: Begin in agreement and stay in agreement.

This is a very old rule of persuasion. Eighty years ago, Dale Carnegie explained it in his book *How to Win Friends and Influence People:*

> In talking to people, don't begin by discussing the things on which you differ. Begin by emphasizing—and keep on emphasizing—the things on which you agree. Keep emphasizing, if possible, that you are both striving for the same end and that your only difference is one of method and not of purpose.

Start every argument from a point of agreement and then give your audience a bridge from their preconceptions to your solutions. The goal is not to change people's minds, it is to show your listeners that you both agree already.

In order to make a progressive argument, we virtually always have to get past the brain's instantaneous System 1 and engage the thoughtful System 2. You need your listeners' minds to reflect on your argument, not react to it. When you begin in agreement, it both demonstrates that you're on their side and helps your audience listen with the calm and rational aspects of their minds.

Finding a point of agreement is not so difficult. You can start by identifying a fairly universally-accepted problem: "Prescription drugs cost too much." Or by empathizing with your listeners' concerns: "You are right to be worried about what this proposed new bridge is going to mean to our community." Or by stating a policy ideal: "Every child in our city should have access to world-class public schools."

To be clear: we are not asking you to obfuscate or misrepresent your views. You never have to compromise your political principles to begin in agreement, you just need to consider a wider range of possibilities. For example:

- If your listener is complaining about taxes (even in a conservative fashion), agree that our tax system is unfair.
- If your audience is worried about government budgets (even when they're no current problem), agree that our government has an obligation to be careful with taxpayer money.
- If someone is concerned about crime (even in a low-crime community), agree that personal safety must be a top priority for government.

- If an individual thinks the neighborhood is going downhill (even if that doesn't seem to be the case), agree that we need to preserve the quality of life.

When you give a speech, find out ahead of time what concerns your audience has. If you don't know in advance, keep your remarks short and allow more time for Q&A. The questioners will tell you what they care about and you'll learn a lot about your community's needs, which will benefit both you and them. When you are in a conversation, listen carefully to what others say—they will provide you with opportunities to agree. Skip the parts where you flatly disagree and steer the discussion toward the elements where you're on the same side. Demonstrate over and over that you understand the problem, that you empathize with your audience, and that you share the same policy ideals.

You may wonder: Where do I take the discussion from there? What about facts and statistics? What about our progressive solutions?

Starting in agreement and speaking from your values does not mean that you can't talk about specific issues. In fact, the agreement and values "stick" more when attached to an issue.

For example, let us say you are talking about making taxes more progressive. Start in agreement, like this:

Say . . .

Our tax system is unfair. The tax burden on working families has increased while rich people and powerful corporations pocket more and more tax giveaways. And that's unjust.

Almost nobody disagrees with that. Then you might provide a statistic or, better yet, tell a story that illustrates the issue and finish with a very brief explanation of how your policy is consistent with those statements of shared belief and how it addresses the problem.

Whatever you do, never say—and try to avoid even implying—that the listeners are wrong. Your audience will stop listening. Similarly, never let your own emotions do the talking. When you are about to speak in anger, take a deep breath and shake it off. Voicing your emotions will make you feel good—you'll get a shot of dopamine in your brain—but it will almost certainly end your opportunity to persuade.

Second: Use progressive values.

Values are words with positive meanings built into them. Words like trustworthy, loyal, helpful, friendly, courteous and kind are values that describe personal behavior. But more than that, they implicitly communicate that the behavior is admirable. You could describe the same conduct as *brave* or *foolhardy*, you could call a person *thrifty* or *penny-pinching*. By choosing to use the value brave over foolhardy or thrifty over penny-pinching, you are framing the behavior as positive.

In politics, values are ideals that describe the kind of society we are trying to build. When you use progressive values, you communicate two things. First, because values are, by definition, beliefs that we share with our listeners, you are starting and staying in agreement with your audience. Values suggest that, whatever the specific policy, your overall goals are the same.

Second, if you understand how to use them, progressive values allow you to describe a consistent political philosophy using concepts that every voter can grasp. (See Chapter 5.)

The stereotypical conservative values are small government, low taxes, free markets, strong military and traditional families. These few words do a pretty good job of laying out a popular philosophy. When conservative values are stated this way, our side too often has no effective response.

Progressives usually want to answer the conservative approach not with our own values but with a laundry list of policies. Or, when we do use values, they tend to evoke negative stereotypes about bleeding-heart liberals: compassion, cooperation, and concern for our fellow citizens. These may appeal to our base, but they do not persuade undecided Americans.

There's another way. It is a set of political values that are poll-tested and proven to work.

When you're talking about an issue where government has no proper role—like free speech, privacy, reproductive rights or religion—declare your commitment to *freedom* or use a similar value from the chart below. When you discuss an issue where government should act as a referee between competing interests—like court proceedings, wages, benefits, subsidies, taxes or education—explain that your position is based on *opportunity* or a value from that column. When you argue about an issue where government should act as a protector—like crime, retirement, health care, zoning or the environment—stand for *security* or a similar value.

Family of Progressive Values

Freedom or similar values: ↓	Opportunity or similar values: ↓	Security or similar values ↓
• Liberty	• Equal opportunity	• Safety; protection
• Privacy	• Justice; equal justice	• Quality of life
• Basic rights	• Fairness; fair share	• Employment security
• Fundamental rights	• Level playing field	• Retirement security
• Religious freedom	• Every American	• Health security

Moreover, put these values together and explain that you stand for *freedom, opportunity and security for all*. This phrase polls better than conservative values, and more important, it's an accurate description of what we stand for. The right wing favors these principles but only for some—the affluent. Progressives insist on providing freedom, opportunity and security to each and every American.

Imagine you are a state legislator visiting constituents door-to-door and you are asked what you're going to do to clean up the stream that runs through a particular neighborhood. And cleaning up that stream is not really the state legislature's job.

A typical progressive might launch into an explanation of the clean water legislation he or she supports. A particularly inept one might say the stream is the responsibility of the city or county and there's little the state can do. A good communicator would start in agreement:

Say . . .

It's a terrible shame that our stream has deteriorated like that. It's unsafe, it's unhealthy, it's wrong for our community.

Why . . .

The only way to connect with this resident is to agree wholeheartedly. Note that you should call it *our* stream and *our* community, even when you live in a different neighborhood. If you can, go on to say you remember what the stream was like when it was clean and beautiful. Then describe your positive values, your goals:

Say . . .

I believe the state needs to make it a top priority to ensure cleaner streams and safer parklands. We need to protect the quality of life in our community.

Why . . .

These are values that you share with every voter: *cleaner*, *safer*, and a *better quality of life*. At this point you are welcome to explain your clean water legislation but keep it simple; you have probably already won a friend. The average voter is really only listening for one thing: Are you on my side? By using values that you share with your listener, you demonstrate that you are.

Every time you have the opportunity to speak to a persuadable audience, don't forget to express your values. Even if listeners grumble about your policy solution, you might very well win their support if you have made clear that you share the same concerns and are trying to achieve the same goals.

Third: Show listeners how they benefit.

Progressives favor policies that benefit society at large. We want to help the underdog. We wish that a majority of Americans were persuaded, as we are, by appeals to the common good. But they aren't.

In fact, it's quite difficult to convince average citizens to support a policy that appears to benefit people other than themselves, their families and their friends. Celinda Lake, one of our movement's very best pollsters, explains that "our culture is very, very individualistic." When faced with a proposed government policy, "people look for themselves in the proposal. People want to know what the proposal will do for me and to me."

That means, whenever possible, you need to show voters that they personally benefit from your progressive policies. Usually that's not so hard. When talking about climate change, emphasize how it affects the listeners' children and grandchildren. When arguing for criminal justice reform, show how it makes us all safer.

Sometimes it's more of a challenge. For example, if you're arguing for programs that benefit people in poverty, do not focus on the way your proposal directly helps the poor, instead find a way that it indirectly benefits the middle class. Persuadable voters are rarely in poverty themselves and they will relate better to an argument aimed at them.

For example, when you argue for an increase in the minimum wage:

Say . . .

Raising the minimum wage puts money in the pockets of hardworking Americans who will spend it on the things they need. This, in turn, generates business for our economy and eases the burden on taxpayer-funded services. It's a win-win. Raising the minimum wage helps build an economy that works for everyone, not just the rich.

Why . . .

Every progressive policy benefits the middle class, often directly but at least indirectly. In contrast, nearly every right-wing policy hurts the middle class, even if it more directly hurts the poor. Since persuadable voters are nearly always in the middle class and they want to know how policies affect them personally, you must tell them.

That does not mean you can explain your positions without mentioning program beneficiaries. In fact, the example above mentions them. The important thing is to connect with persuadable voters and frame the beneficiaries, in one way or another, as deserving.

Americans are not very kind to the poor. Outside of the progressive base, a lot of voters assume that people in poverty failed to help themselves, don't take advantage of opportunities "given to them" and they should "pull themselves up by their bootstraps." Unfortunately, you cannot argue voters out of this belief. So, when you talk about lower-income Americans, you need to go out of your way to describe them as deserving the same chance to succeed as everybody else.

By telling Americans how a policy benefits them, you are once again staying in agreement and demonstrating that you are on their side.

3. Five Mistakes in Persuasion

First: Don't repeat the opponents' frame.

In his book *Don't Think of an Elephant,* Professor George Lakoff provides the most basic principle of framing: "Do not use their language. Their language picks out a frame—and it won't be the frame you want."

Right wing groups spend millions of dollars on message framing. They commission polls, dial groups and focus groups to test words and phrases, and distribute their poll-tested advice to candidates, interest groups and activists. Then right wingers persistently repeat that language, e.g., class warfare, death tax, job creators, nanny state, pro-life, tax relief, union boss, and values voter.

Listen for the right-wing framing and do not repeat those phrases. Throughout this book, we suggest progressive language to substitute. But in addition, go beyond the words and reframe the ideas; change the debate to something larger or more crucial where progressives hold the advantage.

For example, right wingers want to talk about "border security," asserting that it's an emergency. Instead of pointing out the truth, that the number of so-called "migrants" is far below the record pace set during the George W. Bush Administration, argue that the real problem is that we need a comprehensive reform of the federal immigration system—which Americans agree with but our opponents won't even acknowledge.

When conservatives bring up yet another measure to lower taxes for wealthy special interest groups, don't limit the debate to that narrow legislation. Instead, point out the need to rein in a wide range of unfair subsidies and tax breaks enjoyed by the rich and powerful—a subject where Americans overwhelmingly side with us.

When the oil and gas industry pushes for more and bigger pipelines, don't allow the discussion to be limited to a simplistic question of yes or no. Climate change is real; we can and must address it now. For our children and grandchildren and the future security of our nation, we need to focus on developing renewable energy. These are arguments that cannot be effectively denied.

The easiest and best way to reframe our opponents' arguments is by introducing proactive legislation at the federal, state and local levels, which address the same issues as the right-wing talking points. The answer to supposed voter fraud is a comprehensive progressive bill to make voting both secure and more accessible. The response to gun violence is not everyone walking around armed, but our own bill that keeps guns out of the wrong hands. The solution to high prescription drug prices is not "the market," but our own innovative legislation.

In short, progressives need to drive bold, proactive agendas in states and localities, especially in the ones controlled by conservatives, because that's the best way to reframe the debate. Don't fight on our opponents' chosen grounds. Both legislatively and linguistically, the best defense is a good offense.

Second: Don't use language that triggers a negative emotional response.

If you want to persuade, don't tell listeners they are wrong. If you do, they will respond emotionally, and you've lost them. For example, if you're speaking to someone who believes the speed limit is too high, water service costs too much, or voter fraud is rampant, don't directly disagree. Instead, find a point where you do agree, e.g., traffic safety is essential, utilities must be affordable, and our elections must be free, fair and accessible to all qualified voters.

Beyond that kind of direct disagreement, you can also trigger a negative emotional response by evoking the wrong picture in people's heads.

As you surely know, due to decades of messaging by conservatives and complicity by some Democrats, there is a strong stigma attached to the word "welfare." Don't use the term because it will elicit an emotional reaction in many moderate-to-conservative leaning voters. They will think of so-called welfare queens, people who are perceived as lazy and/or cheaters.

Avoid talking about giving benefits or granting rights, which implies special treatment. Instead, say that we should not *deny* protections, which implies that everyone is entitled. You can also talk about treating people fairly or protecting equal opportunity for all.

Using language that elicits positive emotions is not really all that hard. Without expensive focus groups, liberals of the '60s and '70s brilliantly framed programs as the Peace Corps, Head Start, Model Cities, Fair Housing, Equal Employment Opportunity, and the Clean Air Act. In recent years, progressives have found success with positive frames like clean cars, clean elections, clean power, environmental justice, fair pay, fair share health care, health care for all, high road economics, living wage and smart growth.

Look before you leap; think before you speak.

Third: Avoid the passive voice, unless you're trying to cover up.

Richard Nixon and his press secretary were famously ridiculed for saying "mistakes were made." And yet, the same phrase has been used by Democrats and Republicans ever since.

To many people, the passive voice seems like a great way to avoid responsibility. E.g., "the deadline was missed," "the wrong email was sent," or as Justin Timberlake's agent said, "I am sorry if anyone was offended by the wardrobe malfunction during the halftime performance."

But speaking that way is a lousy way to present your case for social change. For example:

Don't say . . .	Say . . .
• Five-thousand people lost their jobs at Walmart.	• Walmart fired 5,000 loyal hardworking employees to increase profits for the owners.
• One-hundred Sam's Club stores were closed.	• Walmart closed 100 Sam's Club stores, laying off thousands of hardworking employees.
• One-hundred demonstrators were arrested.	• At the instruction of the mayor, police illegally arrested 100 peaceful protesters.
• The new law ends health insurance for 50,000.	• The legislature and governor took away healthcare coverage from 50,000 citizens of our state.

Why . . .

When you're speaking about politics or policy, it is essential to show how you and your side are different from the opponents. It's not enough to convey "I am on your side," you have to demonstrate that the political opponents are against their side.

Whenever possible, be proactive in both language and deed.

Fourth: Don't use wonky or insider language.

All too often, progressives assume the person we're talking to knows what we know and thinks the way we do. So, we tend to use the same language to communicate with nonpolitical people that we use to talk with each other. Yet, persuadable Americans aren't like us. They're the least interested in politics and least aware of the facts behind public policy. Persuadables simply don't speak our language.

In talking to our less-politically aware fellow citizens, progressive policymakers and advocates tend to make two errors.

First, progressives often use insider language instead of plain English. Policymakers and advocates tend to speak the technical language of lobbying and carry on a never-ending conversation about bills from the past, measures under consideration and current law. You probably realize that most Americans don't know anything about CBO scoring or Third Reader or the Rules Committee. But average voters also don't know an amendment from a filibuster. Insiders tend to use abbreviations freely, like ENDA for the Employment Non-Discrimination Act or TABOR when talking about a Taxpayer Bill of Rights. They refer to SB 234, PAYGO rules, the ag community and the Hyde amendment. This is a tough habit to break.

Insider jargon serves a useful purpose. It is shorthand that allows those who understand to communicate more efficiently. But it is also a means to be exclusive, to separate members from nonmembers of the club. That's exactly why such language is pernicious; you can't expect persuadable voters to understand a language that was designed, in part, to exclude them.

Second, progressives often use ideological language even though persuadables are the opposite of ideologues. You should not complain of *corporate greed* because persuadable Americans don't have a problem with corporations. You should not say *capitalism* or any *ism* because most Americans don't relate to ideology. Don't say *neo-* or *crypto-* anything! Like technical policy language, ideological language is a form of shorthand. But to persuadable voters, this just sounds like the speaker isn't one of them.

You need to accept persuadable voters as they are, not as you wish they were. They don't know what you know. Use their language and you will be better understood and more likely to be accepted as one of them.

Fifth: Don't overuse facts and statistics.

Progressives embrace facts—the more, the better. That's important in governing but less effective in public persuasion. Advocates will pack a speech with alarming facts and figures like: "30 million Americans are uninsured;" or "one in five children live in poverty;" or "32 million Americans have been victims of racial profiling." When you speak this way, you are assuming that listeners would be persuaded—and policy would change—if only everybody knew what you know.

But that's not how it works. Politics is not a battle of information; it is a battle of ideas. Facts, by themselves, don't persuade. Statistics, especially, must be used sparingly or listeners will just go away confused. Your argument should be built upon ideas and values that the persuadable voters already hold dear.

If you're addressing an audience, a few well-placed facts will help illustrate why the progressive solution is essential, while too many facts will diminish the effectiveness of your argument. If you're speaking one-on-one or in a small group, let your listeners ask for more facts. When people do that, they're helping you persuade them.

Stories are usually more persuasive than statistics. Humans are much more comfortable and familiar with learning lessons from stories. The Bible is full of stories. As children, we learn from fairy tales and mythology. Much of the news is delivered through anecdotes. Our hearts are always ready to embrace a hero or turn against a villain.

4. The Politics of Race, Class and Group Identification

As a candidate and as President, Donald Trump has overtly played whites against people of color. He has vocally attacked Latinos, Muslims, African Americans and Asians.

Among too many examples to cite here, Trump called for limiting immigration from countries that are majority Muslim and for building a wall between the USA and Mexico. He called Black football players sons of bitches, and refused to condemn white nationalists, saying they were defending their "heritage" after one them drove his car into a crowd of counter-protesters and killed a woman.

While Trump has said these things without restraint, he was just expressing the more veiled right-wing narrative of grievance against nonwhites that has been repeated for decades and which greatly increased in volume during the presidency of Barack Obama.

There is science behind this kind of persuasion. Psychology tells us that a great deal of average people's self-image comes from their social identity—the group or groups that they see themselves as a part of.

Social identity divides the world into us and them—the in-group and the out-group. The us can be something as unimportant as which football team a person supports. It can be about an individual's social class or family, college or country. Being part of the group makes people feel good inside. It enhances pride and self-esteem, and usually there's nothing wrong with that.

But people also enhance their self-image by denigrating *them*. Individuals can feel good emotionally by blaming, being prejudiced against, or discriminating against their out-group. Obviously, this kind of politics can very quickly turn ugly.

The question is, how should progressives respond to this enormously important challenge? We offer two main pieces of advice. First, tackle race head on and in connection with class and economic populism. As the nation becomes more divided, there are a growing number of Americans of all races who are troubled by it and who want to see more equitable policy solutions. Second, watch your language carefully to make sure you do not reinforce the notion that everything is a zero-sum game. For decades, the other side has used the trope that if we expand rights and implement policies for people of color, whites will get less.

Both race and class are essential in a progressive narrative

If there is one certainty about the foreseeable political future, it's that the right wing will appeal to bigotry. Politicians will engage in both overt and "dog whistle" appeals to racism, sexism and religious intolerance. Even when a given conservative candidate runs without appeals to prejudice, right-wing PACs and third parties will supply the dirt.

Appeals to bigotry cannot be ignored. Polling has found both our progressive base and persuadable voters agree that talking about race is necessary to move forward toward greater equality, a position that conservatives reject. Use an opening like this:

Say . . .

We all want a better life for our children, whether we are white, black, or brown, fifth generation or newcomer. My opponent says some families have value and some don't. He wants to pit us against each other to gain power for himself and more money for his donors.

If you're not comfortable with direct language, craft something that works better for you. For example, say that our side "puts the interests of working people first, whether white, Black, or brown." Doing so resonates more strongly with persuadables than simply articulating a positive agenda. And explicitly state that right wingers are trying to "pit us against each other" for their own benefit.

Here are two poll-tested narratives that combine issues of race and class. First:

Say . . .

We all work hard for our families, no matter where we come from or what color we are. But, today, there are politicians and greedy lobbyists who hurt all of us by lining the pockets of the rich, defunding our schools, and threatening our seniors with cuts to Medicare and Social Security. Then they turn around and blame poor families, Black people and new immigrants, as though it's their own fault they're struggling to make ends meet. We need to join together—all of us—to fight for our future. That's how we won better wages, safer workplaces, and civil rights. And that's how we can elect new leaders who work for all of us, not just the wealthy few.

And second:

Say . . .

America's strength comes from our ability to work together—to come together from different places and different races into one nation. For this to be a place of freedom for all, we can't let anyone pit us against each other based on what someone looks like, where they come from, or how much money they have. It's time to stand up for each other and choose leaders who reflect the very best of America. Together, we can make this a place where freedom and opportunity are for everyone, no exceptions.

Such language isn't going to change the minds of people who are racist and/or who support policies that more deeply enshrine systemic or structural racism. But it can move persuadable Americans who already have some understanding that they're being manipulated by racially charged language or policies. Perhaps more important, it energizes people in the progressive base who are organizing to hold elected officials accountable and to create a more egalitarian country.

Donald Trump's own economic message, directed at non-college educated whites, is that conservatives side with them while progressives side only with people of color. We can and must take back the economic narrative—progressives side with both the middle class and low-income Americans, as well as with people of color—while conservatives side with the rich.

Current economic reality

The media continually reassure us that the economy is good, the stock market is strong, and unemployment and inflation are low. And yet, while the rich are getting much richer, average American families are barely getting by. About 60 percent of Americans are living paycheck-to-paycheck; more than 40 percent couldn't pay for an unexpected expense of $400; on average, credit card holders are carrying negative balances of more than $8,000; and students are leaving college tens of thousands of dollars in debt. In short, only the top 5-to-10 percent of Americans are economically secure. But why?

As demonstrated by the following chart, the long-term benefits of increased productivity—that is, the creation of wealth across the U.S. economy—were fairly distributed to average workers from the post-war period into the Nixon Administration.

Disconnect between productivity and a typical worker's compensation, 1948–2015

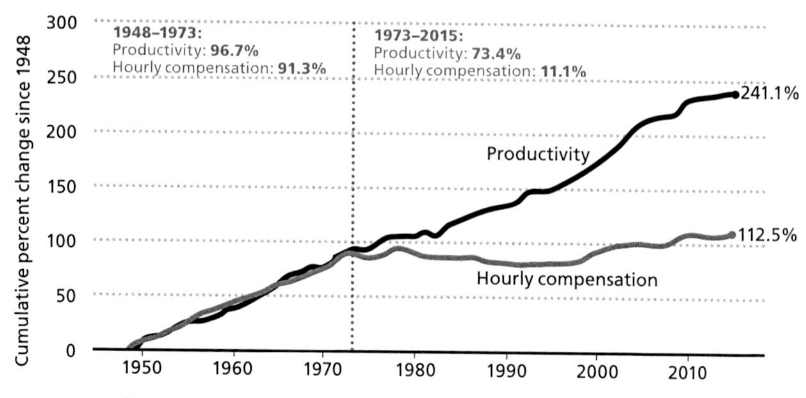

Source: Economic Policy Institute (2016)

But starting in the 1970s and greatly accelerating during the Reagan Administration, real compensation (that is, wages and benefits, adjusted for inflation) stopped rising. While the economy continued to grow at a rapid pace, typical workers no longer received a reasonable share of the wealth they helped to create. Instead, nearly all of that money was, and still is, diverted to the most affluent.

This can also be seen another way. The chart below demonstrates that since the end of the Reagan Administration, the richest 10 percent of Americans doubled their wealth while the bottom 90 percent gained only slightly, and the bottom half—which own just one percent of all the nation's assets—gained nothing.

Holdings of Family Wealth

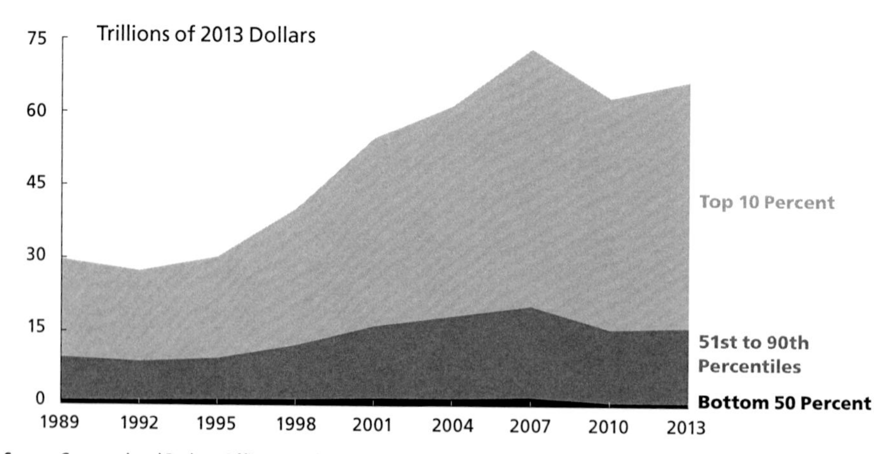

Source: Congressional Budget Office, *Trends in Family Wealth* (2016)

Today, the richest one-tenth of one percent of Americans (fewer than 200,000 families) own about the same amount of private wealth as the bottom 90 percent (about 110 million families) combined. The three wealthiest Americans own more assets than the entire bottom half of the U.S. population. And just 26 people own as much wealth as half of the world's population (that is, 3.8 billion people) combined.

While conservatives assert it was just normal functioning of "the market," the redirection of wealth to the wealthy was consciously accomplished in myriad ways, large and small. Management pay was exponentially increased, workers' benefits were minimized, key government regulations were amended or abolished, taxes were evaded, unions were destroyed, corporations sent factory jobs overseas, businesses cut costs by minimizing customer service and instead making their customers do part of the work, and most recently, Wall Street embraced money-making schemes that were little more than scams. The wealth that all Americans created together didn't just passively flow to the rich, they actively took it for themselves.

If this sounds to you like a harsh assessment, we urge you to read about it yourself. It is essential to understand what underlies the populist uprising that fueled both the Trump and Sanders campaigns in 2016. Without knowing any of the details of these charts and statistics, typical American workers feel that they have been treated unfairly, that their families are worse off than they were some decades ago, and *somebody is to blame for it.* And, in that at least, they are right.

Obviously the right-wing media, owned by and operated for the rich, are not going to talk about this concentration of wealth. But neither will the mainstream media. Thus, the economic truth is both unseen and unheard—it remains hidden in plain sight—and, as such, it can trigger Americans to blame people of color, immigrants, low income workers, and others, rather than the real culprits.

The Progressive Narrative

For at least a decade, virtually every poll has shown that, if they hear the argument, persuadable voters will agree that the rich deserve blame. For example, among American voters:

- By nearly 2-to-1, they believe "the economic system…mainly works to benefit those in power."
- 82 percent say that "wealthy people have too much power and influence in Washington."

- 76 percent think "the wealthiest Americans should pay higher taxes" while only nine percent believe "upper income people...are paying too much."
- 75 percent think "corporations should pay higher taxes" while only eight percent believe "corporations...are paying too much."
- 92 percent agree that "there are already too many special tax loopholes for the wealthiest Americans" and 90 percent agree there are too many "for corporations."

Nevertheless, Barack Obama rarely made this point as President and Hillary Clinton largely avoided it as a candidate. So, the partisan debate on economics—what was heard by voters—was quite one-sided. That simply cannot continue.

This is an easy message to deliver because Americans already believe our narrative, if only we will say it. And there are many ways to communicate it effectively. For example:

Say . . .

For most working Americans, our economy is broken. To fix it, our policies must benefit all the people, of every race and ethnicity—not just the richest one percent. Our system works when everyone gets a fair shot, everyone gives their fair share, and everyone plays by the same rules.

Why . . .

Persuadable voters believe in a series of stereotypes about progressives and conservatives. In economic policy, persuadable voters like the concept of a conservative who supports low taxes and free markets. But they also believe that today's conservatives favor the rich rather than the middle class. At the same time, persuadable voters like a progressive who fights for economic fairness. But they also tend to believe that liberals favor the poor over the middle class.

So, pretty obviously, you need to emphasize that conservative policy supports the rich while progressive policy supports the middle class. That does not mean you should lessen your commitment to fight poverty or move your policies to the right, it means you should focus attention on the fact that your economic policies benefit the middle class while conservative policies don't.

The narrative above uses simple, non-ideological language to express that idea. The first sentence expresses agreement. If you know something specific about your audience's economic woes, use it. Do not imply that the economy is okay because you will likely get a very angry response. The third sentence was used by President Obama and polls extremely well.

This is another version of the same theme:

Say . . .

Our economy is upside down. The majority of Americans of every race and ethnicity are struggling, while the rich are doing better than ever. We need an economy that works for Main Street, not Wall Street. Every hardworking American should have the opportunity to earn a decent living, receive high-quality affordable health care, get a great education for their children, and retire with security. [Their right-wing policy] favors the rich, [our progressive policy] sides with the rest of us.

Why . . .

It is important to use language that explicitly blames the rich. A Hart Research poll demonstrated this by asking persuadable voters which candidate they would support in two circumstances. When given a choice between a Republican who "will grow the economy" and a Democrat who "will make the economy work for all of us," these voters chose the Republican by 55-to-45 percent. But when given the choice between a Republican who "will grow the economy" and a Democrat who "will make the economy work for all of us, *not just the wealthy*," they chose the Democrat by 61-to-39 percent. By explicitly indicting the wealthy, the Democrat gained 16 points!

Here are some additional phrases that work:

Say . . .

- Too often the system is rigged to favor the wealthy over ordinary Americans, or big corporations over small businesses.
- It does not have to be that way—we can change the rules.
- We need an economy that works for all of us, not just the wealthy few.
- To build a strong economy, we need a strong middle-class for everyone, of every race.
- It's time to rewrite the economic rules to benefit all Americans, not just the rich and powerful.

Why . . .

These narratives and messages appeal to just about every persuadable voter without sounding ideological. That's important because most voters think that "free enterprise has done more to lift people out of poverty, help build a strong middle class, and make our lives better than all of the government's programs put together." So don't attack capitalism, condemn economic unfairness.

More specifically:

Don't say . . .	**Say . . .**
• Corporations/ businesses are bad • Anything negative about small business	• Wall Street speculators • Unfair tax breaks and giveaways to Wall Street, giant banks, and major corporations • Anything positive about Main Street

Why . . .

Voters feel good about corporations and businesses—most work for one. Voters believe that businesses create jobs and America needs jobs. Americans especially adore the concept of Main Street. And as pollster Celinda Lake says, "Americans are in love with *small business*. It's a concept that voters see as almost synonymous with America." By small business, they mean family-run businesses with five or perhaps ten employees.

Don't say . . .	**Say . . .**
• Income inequality • Economic disparity	• Richest one percent, the super-rich, billionaires • All the rest of us • Economic injustice or unfairness • The disappearing middle class

Why . . .

Understand that the rich, or the major banks and corporations, are not unpopular for who they are, but for what they've done. To be effective, you need to connect the bad guy to the bad deed, such as unfair tax breaks, moving jobs overseas, accepting bailouts, or paying outrageous CEO bonuses. Americans expect some people to earn more than others. It's not income inequality that voters oppose, it is economic injustice, economic unfairness and people who cheat or rig the system.

Don't say . . .

- Capitalism
- Free markets, free enterprise, free trade

Say . . .

- The economic system isn't working for working families
- Fair markets, fair trade, level playing field
- Rigging the rules, gaming the system
- Stacking the deck
- An economy that works for all of us

Why . . .

If you attack the market system, you marginalize yourself. In addition, there are a lot of economic phrases that, in the minds of most Americans, may mean something different from what you intend. Don't say *capitalism*, *socialism*, or *fascism* because the far-right has succeeded in confusing voters about their meaning. Don't use the phrases *free markets* or *free enterprise* because, in this context, "free" triggers positive thoughts about conservative economics.

And yet, you should explicitly support a fair market system. You need to draw a distinction between conservative anything-goes economics and a progressive system that enforces basic rules-of-the-road to level the playing field and keep markets honest and fair for everyone.

The argument for capitalism is that by harnessing individuals' economic drive, all of society is enriched by their hard work and innovation. Progressives are for that. But society does not win—in fact, it loses—when people get rich by gaming the system, by exploiting tax or regulatory loopholes, by dismantling viable companies, or by creating scams that aren't technically illegal but should be.

Conservatives relentlessly warp markets to benefit the rich and powerful. They use subsidies, loopholes, trade policy, labor law and economic complexity to corrupt markets. It is progressives who seek to build *fair markets*. Help voters visualize such a system.

Say . . .

We need an economy that's fair to everyone, whether Black, white or brown. That means structuring a system that not only rewards people for hard work and innovation, but also discourages people from gaming the system or passing costs on to the community. We need rules of the road that make economic competition fair, open and honest. A fair market system energizes our economy, creates jobs, and allows every American to pursue the American Dream.

Why . . .

When you talk about the American Dream—fair pay, health insurance, homeownership, education, retirement security—it provides the opportunity to explain that none of this is possible without a change in direction. It lays out an overarching goal; only progressive policy will ever get us any closer to turning that Dream into a reality.

Finally, when talking about economics, don't limit the conversation to income inequality. In our country, the biggest inequalities involve assets.

Say . . .

Our economic system should reward hard work and innovation. That's the American way. But right now, the richest one percent in America own more wealth than the bottom 90 percent of Americans combined. The rich don't need more subsidies and loopholes. They need to pay their fair share.

5. The Philosophy of Progressive Values

The overall purpose of our message framing books and materials is to show you—a policymaker, activist, advocate, campaigner, candidate, or political observer—how to persuade others. Our focus on political *values* is practical—it works.

But that does not mean that progressives should choose their values randomly. The fact is, progressive values describe an overall political philosophy. Let us take a few steps back and describe what kind of philosophy progressives need, how a values-based philosophy operates, and why it is persuasive.

In a glorious poem, Langston Hughes evoked the spirit of the American dream. It is our soaring common vision:

> *Let America be America again.*
> *Let it be the dream it used to be.*
> *Let it be the pioneer on the plain*
> *Seeking a home where he himself is free.*
>
> *Let America be the dream the dreamers dreamed—*
> *Let it be that great strong land of love*
> *Where never kings connive nor tyrants scheme*
> *That any man be crushed by one above.*

What you should understand is that the American dream is *not* about a society where government secures the greatest good for the greatest number. Our dream is personal. It's about a poor child delivering newspapers and one day ending up as the publisher. It's about an unskilled worker attending night school and becoming a successful manager. It's about individuals and families practicing their religion without interference, getting ahead through hard work, and being able to retire in security and comfort.

The American dream is a prayer, a vision, a fervent hope that every individual in our nation may be given a fair chance to build a successful life. This deeply held, deeply felt common vision for our nation is both about money—individuals and their families getting ahead, and about self-determination—individuals and their families deciding what to think and how to live. Our dream celebrates the individual.

American individualism goes way back. If you took political science in college, you may recall that Alexis de Tocqueville, observing the America of 1831, was impressed (but not favorably) by our individualism. Even earlier, Benjamin Franklin—the quintessential self-made man—reflected the thinking of his era, "The U.S. Constitution doesn't guarantee happiness, only the pursuit of it. You have to catch up with it yourself." Thomas Jefferson initially made individualism an explicit part of the Declaration of Independence. His first draft stated that "all men are created equal and independent." The founding fathers' dedication to individualism led them to make the Bill of Rights a centerpiece of American government. And throughout the history of our nation, despite great hardships, immigrants traveled here (those who came voluntarily), settlers moved across the plains, and farmers migrated to cities, all to find a better life for themselves and their families. America has been shaped by this common quest of individual Americans.

Individualism is our nation's greatest strength and its greatest weakness. It drives innovation and progress, but it also consigns millions of Americans to lives spent in poverty. In fact, the poem "Let America Be America Again" is primarily about workers in the fields, the mines, and the factories whose American dreams were crushed. The system doesn't work for many or most because of our national culture of competition.

Competition is the very bedrock of our governmental, economic, and social systems. Elections and court cases are competitions. School and college are competitions. Our economy is a complex and gigantic competition. Even our ideas of style—attractive clothes, jewelry, furniture, houses—are based on how they compare with others. Obviously, where there is competition there are both winners and losers.

The point is, we can't force a communalistic philosophy on an individualistic nation. Let's be clear. The progressive-liberal-Democratic base of voters would gladly accept and espouse a communitarian philosophy. We all wish that American culture were more oriented toward altruism and community. But it isn't. A realistic progressive philosophy is one that accepts our national culture of individualism and competition and—nevertheless—seeks to make the American dream accessible to all. How can we envision such a philosophy?

Balance Is Justice

Imagine a balance scale—the old-fashioned kind with two pans, one suspended from each end of a bar. It's the kind of scale that symbolizes equal justice under law. In a progressive world, the role of government is to help balance the scale when powerful individuals or organizations compete against weaker ones. Government should function as a counterweight on the scale of justice. The greater the disparity of power between competing interests, the greater weight the government must provide to the weaker side.

It is not government's job to ensure that everyone wins every competition—that would be a logical impossibility. Instead, government must ensure that, whenever possible, competition is both fair and humane. In other words, *justice* is the purpose of government, and in an individualistic society, *balance* is the means of achieving justice.

A system in balance rewards hard work, efficiency, and innovation—which benefit all of society, and discourages crime, corruption, and schemes to game the system—which rob all of society. As a practical matter, despite all efforts, our system will never be perfectly in balance. Justice is a journey not a destination. But we can switch this mighty country onto the right track and open up the throttle to increase its speed.

You may be thinking: Isn't balance an awfully broad principle? How do we apply it?

Here is how. We break down public policy into three situations, where: (1) government has no proper role; (2) government acts as a referee; and (3) government acts as a protector.

Freedom

FIRST, where government has no proper role, because public action would violate individual rights, progressive policy should be based on freedom. By *freedom,* we mean the absence of legal interference with our fundamental rights—freedom of speech, religion, and association; the right to privacy; the rights of the accused; and the right of all citizens to vote. Compared to an individual, government wields tremendous power, so a progressive policy adds great weight—in the form of strong legal rights—to the individual's side of the scale. For example, freedom of speech is absolutely sacrosanct unless it immediately and directly puts others in danger—"falsely shouting fire in a theater" as Justice Oliver Wendell Holmes put it.

Freedom should be fairly easy to understand—it's a defense of our basic constitutional rights and civil liberties. We include the right to vote because it should be as sacred as any constitutional right. The very definition of *democracy*—rule by the people—requires the unrestricted right to vote. So, laws that keep American citizens from casting ballots should be eliminated on the grounds that they violate our most fundamental democratic freedom.

We intentionally adopt a limited definition of freedom, often called "negative freedom." Why? That's the only way it works. When defined too broadly, freedom becomes an empty platitude that can be wielded as a bludgeon to pummel any side of any political argument.

Freedom is the cornerstone of America's value system. For two centuries, America has been defined by its commitment to freedom. One poll found that Americans believe—by a margin of 73 to 15 percent—that *freedom* is more important than *equality.* But because it's so popular, *freedom* is the most misused of all political terms.

For nearly 20 years, conservatives have proclaimed that both the wars in Iraq and Afghanistan, and the "war on terror," were and are in defense of our freedom. But it's not true. Our freedom was never in jeopardy—the Iraqis, the Taliban, ISIS and al-Qaeda, none of them attempted to invade America and control our government. U.S. military and police actions might be said to protect our security, but not our freedom. So don't use the word *freedom* when discussing current military adventures—it just provides a false justification for war.

Similarly, conservatives equate freedom with capitalism. But it's not true. Our nation's market economy is not free from government control—actually, it is dominated by government. Markets are based on a dense web of laws enforced by multiple layers of federal, state, and local agencies. Businesses are not free to sell diseased meat, make insider stock trades, pollute our air and water, or discriminate on the basis of race, gender, or ethnicity. So don't be fooled by the terms *free market, free enterprise,* or *free trade,* because they all support right-wing policies.

Most astonishing is the way religious extremists use the word *freedom* to mean the very opposite. They argue that freedom gives them the right to use the power of government to impose their religious views on the rest of us. When they pressure school boards to mandate the teaching of intelligent design in schools, when they erect monuments to the Ten Commandments on public property, when they work to ban all abortions, when they seek to promote prayer in public schools, right-wingers assert it's an exercise in religious freedom. But it's simply not true. Freedom is the *absence* of government intervention.

Dear friends, we have a solemn responsibility to fiercely guard our constitutional and human rights to freedom. We must use freedom as our bully pulpit when arguing that government is out of control. We must point out that freedom is one of our most cherished values. We must insist that Clarence Darrow was right when he said, "You can protect your liberties in this world only by protecting the other man's freedom. You can be free only if I am free."

Opportunity

SECOND, where government acts as a referee between private, unequal interests, progressive policy should be based on opportunity. By *opportunity,* we mean a level playing field in social and economic affairs—fair dealings between the powerful and the less powerful, the elimination of discrimination, and a quality education for all. Competing interests usually hold unequal power, so progressive policy adds weight—guarantees of specific protections—to the weaker interest. For example, unskilled low-wage workers have no leverage to bargain for higher pay. That's why it is up to the government to impose a reasonable minimum wage. Quite simply, when social and market forces do not naturally promote equal opportunity, government must step in.

Opportunity means, more than anything, a fair marketplace. Although progressives tend to stress the rights of consumers and employees against businesses, opportunity also means fairness between businesses—especially helping small enterprises against large ones—and fairness for stockholders against corporate officers. Individual ambition, innovation, and effort—harnessed by the market system—are supposed to benefit society as a whole. But that can happen only when the competition is fair.

Opportunity also means fair economic transactions with the government. Government should use the scale of justice when determining taxes—obviously a sliding scale where those who have the least pay the least. And when it is the government that is making payments—for contracts, subsidies, public education, and the like—the principle of opportunity dictates that all individuals and companies should have equal access, unless the balance of justice demands a measure of affirmative action.

The concept of opportunity is an easy sell to progressives. And yet, since the Reagan years, we've been losing the struggle to the right wingers who flatly oppose opportunity.

Conservatives have fought against ending discrimination, even though equal treatment is a precondition for equal opportunity. They don't even pretend to support equal opportunity in commerce; instead, conservatives lobby for government favors, no-bid contracts, and economic development giveaways. And right-wingers seek to destroy anything that allows individuals to stand up to larger economic forces, with labor unions, consumer protections, and antimonopoly policies under constant attack.

Our mission is clear. It is to guarantee that all Americans are able to realize their goals through education, hard work, and fair pay. We must provide

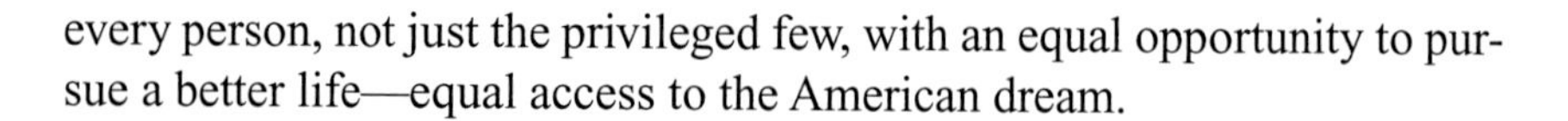

every person, not just the privileged few, with an equal opportunity to pursue a better life—equal access to the American dream.

Security

THIRD, where government acts to protect those who cannot reasonably protect themselves, including future generations, progressive policy should be based on security. By *security,* we mean protecting Americans from domestic criminals and foreign terrorists, of course, but also insuring the sick and the vulnerable, safeguarding the food we eat and products we use, and preserving our environment.

There is always a threat that larger or unexpected forces will attack any one of us, so progressive policy adds weight, in the form of government institutions and programs, that helps protect us from harm. For example, society has a responsibility to protect the elderly, the disabled, widows, and orphans and that's why an aptly named federal program has functioned in that role for more than a half-century—Social Security.

Security can be divided into three categories. First, government should secure our personal safety and health. That includes military and police protection, firefighting, health insurance, medical research, and protection from impurities, pollutants, and hazardous waste. Second, government should perform its fiduciary duty to protect individuals who cannot reasonably protect themselves. That includes people who are poor, elderly, children, disabled, mentally ill—as well as future generations. Of course, the weaker the individual, the greater the protection required. Third, government should protect our common future as a nation. That includes building and maintaining infrastructure, using zoning powers to enhance quality of life, and safeguarding the environment.

Progressives support the concept of security, of course. But we usually detour around the word when talking about law enforcement or national security. Like *freedom,* the word *security* seems to stick in the throats of progressives, perhaps because we're worried we'll sound like conservatives.

Progressives want to jump immediately to collaboration and cooperation, rehabilitation and reeducation. That line of thinking is both destructive and unrealistic. Crime and terrorism are issues of security. Yes, we believe that our policies are the best means to ensure security, but we need to talk about the ends as well. The proper role of government in these matters, and the top priority of officeholders, is to provide security for our communities. To ignore security is to lose the argument.

An American Philosophy

Now that you think about it, don't the principles of freedom, opportunity, and security sound kind of familiar?

> We hold these truths to be self-evident, that all men are created equal, that they are endowed by their Creator with certain unalienable Rights, that among these are Life, Liberty and the pursuit of Happiness.

This famous line from the Declaration of Independence is more than a set of high-sounding platitudes—it is an assertion of American political philosophy. And it's a *progressive* philosophy.

By "Life," Thomas Jefferson and the signers of the Declaration did not mean simply the right to survival, which would suggest that being beaten *almost* to death is okay. They meant a right to personal *security*. By "Liberty," Jefferson was referring to the kinds of *freedoms* that were ultimately written into all federal and state Bills of Rights, blocking the government from infringing upon speech, religion, the press, and trial by jury, as well as protecting individuals from wrongful criminal prosecutions.

And how do we translate Jefferson's "pursuit of Happiness?" It cannot mean that everyone has the God-given right to do whatever makes them happy. Read "happiness" together with the earlier part of the same sentence, "all men are created equal." Jefferson is not saying that people have an unbridled right to pursue happiness; he is saying they have an *equal right* to pursue happiness. In today's language, we'd call that *equal opportunity*.

Here's how these truths might read in updated language: "All of us have an equal right to freedom, opportunity, and security." No one is above the law; everyone is equal under the law. No one is born above anyone else, we're all equal as Americans.

Because we will never live in a perfect world, our job is to move American reality closer to American ideals. Thomas Jefferson wouldn't have expected us to achieve equal access to life, liberty and the pursuit of happiness for all Americans. He would have expected us to try. In fact, we owe that effort to all the founding fathers and all the other brave men and women who risked their lives and sacrificed to make a better country for their fellow citizens.

We progressives haven't forgotten the principles that inspired America. But we have misplaced them. And worse, we've allowed right-wing extremists to hijack our ideals and wave them like a flag, rallying Americans to their distinctly un-American cause. It is time to right that wrong.

Freedom, Opportunity, and Security for All

Let's raise the banner of our progressive philosophy: freedom, opportunity, and security for all.

That means we believe society should step into an unfair competition, balancing the scale to help the weaker interest get a fair deal. It means that where government has no proper role, we demand freedom; where government acts as a referee between economic interests, we champion opportunity; and where government should protect those who cannot protect themselves, we call for security.

Every issue of public policy is encompassed by at least one of our three ideals. Abortion, racial profiling, and voting rights are about freedom. Equal pay, mortgage assistance, and improving public schools are about opportunity. Terrorism, sentencing reform, and universal health care are about security.

In fact, every progressive policy promotes greater freedom, opportunity, or security for everyone. That's the distinction between progressive and conservative. We seek to extend freedom, opportunity, and security to all Americans. They work to limit freedom, opportunity, and security—to redistribute wealth toward the wealthy, power toward the powerful, and privilege toward the privileged.

Without our progressive values, how can we explain what it means to be a progressive? How can we describe the proper role of government? How can we distinguish ourselves in a fundamental way from conservatives? Indeed, progressives can't and don't—and that is why we have so much trouble persuading Americans who really ought to support our cause.

Not coincidentally, "freedom, opportunity and security for all" has been poll-tested (by Lake Research Partners). It is not only our strongest message, it's the only one that defeats the generic conservative message.

So speak loudly and proudly. Our progressive values are the principles that fueled the flame of the American Revolution. The same torch of American ideals was passed from Jefferson to Lincoln, and from TR to FDR to JFK. Seize the moral high ground. Show how we are the true American patriots, how we are the ones who see the best direction for our country and its residents, and how we will fight for our ideals—and ultimately win.

SECTION TWO

HOW TO TALK ABOUT PROGRESSIVE POLICIES

HOW TO TALK ABOUT PROGRESSIVE POLICIES

6. Civil Rights & Liberties

Begin in agreement, for example: What makes America special is our commitment to freedom and justice for all.

Our values: Freedom, liberty, fundamental rights, fundamental fairness, basic rights, constitutional rights, personal privacy, equal opportunity, fairness, stopping discrimination and government intrusion

Our vision: *Our nation was founded and built upon the self-evident truth that everyone is created equal. That ideal calls us to defend liberty and justice for all people, with no exceptions. In the 21st century, three policies are of foremost importance: (1) outlaw discrimination based on race, gender, age, disability, religion, ethnicity, sexual orientation or gender identity; (2) guarantee fundamental fairness for immigrants; and (3) protect our privacy from government intrusion.*

Civil rights ensure that people will be treated equally regardless of their gender, race, religion, ethnicity, sexual orientation, or any other differentiation that is irrelevant to our inherent rights as residents and citizens. Civil liberties guarantee fundamental human rights that are, or should be, protected by our Constitution.

The individual circumstances that require the protection of civil rights and liberties tend to be unpopular. It's unpopular to defend the rights of criminals. It's often unpopular for a minority to play a role where that group wasn't seen before. Whenever free speech needs to be protected, it is almost certainly unpopular speech, because popular speech isn't attacked.

But even when causes are unpopular, we can defend popular ideals: equal opportunity for civil rights, and freedom for civil liberties.

Let us consider a few examples:

Immigrants

Polls show that there is a tremendous difference in the way Americans feel about unauthorized immigrants depending on whether or not they are perceived as *criminals*. Seventy-eight percent of Americans would "deport all people currently living in the country illegally who have been convicted of other crimes while living in the U.S." (Additional research demonstrates that these must be "serious crimes.") Without being prompted about *criminals*, more than 70 percent say we "should not attempt to deport all people currently living in the country illegally." More specifically, if "illegal immigrants have been in this country for a number of years, hold a job, speak English, and are willing to pay any back taxes that they owe," 90 percent favor allowing them to stay in the U.S. "and eventually allow them to apply for U.S. citizenship."

Say . . .

America is a nation of values, founded on the idea that every one of us has the right to freedom, justice, and fair treatment under our Constitution. The millions of immigrants who have lived in our country for years, who work hard and play by the rules—they make our economy stronger, which benefits all of us. That's why [the solution you advocate]...

Why . . .

Right-wing advocates want to make this debate about crime. Don't help ingrain those ideas by repeating them, and don't use the word *illegal* even to make the entirely truthful statement that "no human is illegal." Unless you are specifically talking about immigrants who may be criminals (e.g. in the debate about *detainers*), assert that you are talking about people with no criminal background.

Nothing you say is going to sway the right-wing base. In a one-on-one conversation, it is futile to keep arguing with an anti-immigrant stalwart. But if persuadable voters are watching you debate the issue, you can take another step and address the real problem: that our immigration system is obsolete.

Say . . .

Our immigration system should be completely fair; it should embody justice. But due to years of gridlock in Washington, that system is a mess. It's time for the Congress to stop playing politics and create an immigration process that recognizes the value of people who have lived here for years, working hard and playing by the rules. We need a system that keeps families together, creates a roadmap for those who aspire to become citizens, and strengthens our economy for decades to come.

Overall, you need to move the conversation away from individual immigrants who are stereotypically portrayed as bad people, to the real problem: a bad immigration process. The word choices in these short examples require some explanation.

Don't say . . .

- Illegal aliens
- Illegal immigrants
- Undocumented immigrants

Say . . .

- New American immigrants
- New Americans
- Aspiring citizens

Why . . .

Don't say *aliens* because that implies they are different from *us*, which is both inaccurate and offensive. Don't say *illegal* because it suggests that they are criminals deserving of punishment, which is false. *Undocumented* has been thoroughly tested and, unfortunately, does not work. If you have to be more specific, you might say *immigrants who are not authorized to be here*. On the positive side, *new American immigrants*, *new Americans* and people who *aspire to be citizens* are poll-tested and move the conversation in a productive direction.

If you are debating the recent increase at our southern border of asylum seekers from El Salvador, Honduras and Guatemala (known as the Northern Triangle, one of the most dangerous places on earth), don't call them "migrants." They are "refugees." Refugees have rights under both U.S. and international law. They are in no way "illegal"—rather, their applications for asylum comply with the law. (Even the mainstream media does not seem to understand that the current families at the border are not the same—nor nearly as many—immigrants as those who came by the millions during the Administration of George W. Bush.)

No matter their legal status, Americans are not inclined to *give* anything to immigrants, but at the same time, they generally don't want to *deny* rights or necessities. So frame your arguments accordingly. For example, if you are arguing for a state DREAM Act to allow the children of new American immigrants to be eligible for in-state tuition rates:

Say . . .

We should reward hard work and responsibility. When young aspiring Americans graduate from a local high school after they have lived here for years and stayed out of trouble, we should not deny them access to college tuition rates that are available to all their graduating classmates. Education is the cornerstone of our democracy and our economy, so when we enable young people to go to college, we all reap the benefits.

Or if you are arguing to allow immigrants access to driver's licenses:

Say . . .

The laws about driving on our highways should be designed to make us all safer. So it doesn't make sense to deny new American immigrants the ability to get a driver's license. We should want them licensed to ensure that every driver on the road is trained, tested and covered by insurance. It's a policy that benefits all of us.

LGBTQIA+ Rights

Most Americans don't understand the inequalities faced by LGBTQIA+ people and how those inequalities affect their lives. Regardless, in just the past few years, Americans have moved rapidly to accept marriage equality and reject discrimination against gay and transgender people.

For example, as recently as 2011, a majority of Americans opposed marriage between same-sex couples and it was still a fairly effective wedge issue for conservatives as recently as 2009. Today, Americans support marriage equality by a margin of 2-to-1.

By an even stronger margin, Americans support LGBT anti-discrimination laws. Almost 70 percent favor and only 24 percent oppose "laws that would protect gay, lesbian, bisexual and transgender people against discrimination in jobs, public accommodations and housing." Even Republicans support such laws by a margin of 56-to-36.

We can continue this heartening trend by pointing out that, when it comes to what's important about being an American, LGBTQIA+ people have the same values as everyone else.

Say . . .

This is about everyday Americans who want the same chance as everyone else to pursue health and happiness, earn a living, be safe in their communities, and take care of the ones they love.

Why . . .

Say that all of us want the same things in life and we should all be treated fairly and equally.

Don't say . . .

- Protect or grant rights
- Benefits
- Civil rights

Say . . .

- Fairness and equality
- Equal opportunity
- Remove unfair barriers

Why . . .

Talking about *rights*, *benefits* or what LGBTQIA+ people *deserve* does not help persuadable voters understand the issues and it tends to sound like you want something different or special for LGBTQIA+ people. Also, civil rights comparisons can alienate some African Americans.

Use language that is inclusive, language that shows unfair barriers prevent LGBTQIA+ people from doing things that we hold dear or even take for granted, like fulfilling obligations to their loved ones, their families, their friends, their neighbors, their communities and their country. Use examples that help Americans acknowledge LGBTQIA+ people as average, hardworking Americans who deserve to be treated as such.

When you are advocating for anti-discrimination statutes, it's essential to understand that Americans are not aware that LGBTQIA+ people can lose their jobs or be denied housing simply because of who they are. You must tell them.

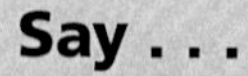

Say . . .

All hardworking people in our community should have the chance to earn a living, provide for themselves and their families, and live like everyone else. But in our state/city, it's currently legal to fire employees or refuse to rent an apartment to people just because they are gay or transgender. Nobody should have to live in fear that they can be fired or evicted just because of who they are.

Why . . .

Most states do not have anti-discrimination laws to protect gay people and fewer still cover transgender people. In states that don't provide protection, it is usually possible for cities and counties to enact their own local laws, and many have already done so.

Don't say . . .

- Employment or housing rights
- Discrimination

Say . . .

- Employment or housing protections
- Treating people fairly and equally
- Equal opportunity

Why . . .

Avoid talking about *giving* or *granting* any *rights*, which implies special treatment. Instead, say that we should not *deny* protections, which implies these rights are inherent to everyone. Obviously, we oppose discrimination, but that language can lead to a polarized debate, so it's better to talk about treating people fairly, or protecting equal opportunity.

Finally, we may be sorely tempted to take some swings at our political opponents, to brand them negatively. But it is better to let them negatively brand themselves

Don't say . . .

- Hate, haters, hatred
- Bigot, bigots, bigotry
- Prejudice
- Religious extremists
- Anti-gay Christians

Say . . .

- Love, standing for love
- Exclusion, rejection and intolerance
- Anti-gay activists
- Radical right activists

Why . . .

When we make clear that we're on the side of love, our opponents are against love. This implication is enough. It's not useful to employ emotionally charged words like haters or bigots, no matter how tempting or true it might be. And we certainly don't want to use language that seems to imply that an entire religious tradition or denomination is anti-gay. You can say *this is the kind of exclusion and intolerance that divides our community* or *the hurtful rhetoric of anti-gay activists*. But generally, stick to the positive and your audience will understand that you believe everyone deserves the same chance at happiness and stability, while our opponents simply do not. For example:

Say . . .

If America stands for anything, it's equal opportunity for all. If you have two children or grandchildren, and one is straight and the other gay, you still love them equally. You know the government should treat them fairly and equally. That is why [explain your policy solution here...]

The Ten Commandments

Hopefully you won't have to debate a proposal to display the Ten Commandments in government buildings. But you might, and we use it here to represent issues where religious advocates seek to impose their religion upon others. And, to understand the difficulty of the progressive position, it is important to realize that Americans favor posting the Ten Commandments in government buildings by a margin of more than 3-to-1.

Say . . .

The Ten Commandments are a moral inspiration and I applaud churches and synagogues that post and teach them. Another inspiration is the First Amendment of the United States Constitution, because it guarantees our most important freedoms. Our country is based on freedom. Hundreds of thousands of Americans have fought and died for our freedom. The First Amendment guarantees the right to display the Ten Commandments everywhere *except* government property—where it is prohibited. To maintain our freedom, this is the rule we must follow.

Why . . .

Freedom is the most powerful word in the American political lexicon. Conservatives understand this and use it—in inappropriate situations—again and again. So when progressives have the opportunity to defend freedom, we must do it explicitly and enthusiastically.

7. CONSUMER PROTECTION

Begin in agreement, for example: We need a marketplace that is fair to everyone.

Our values: Justice, equal justice, civil justice, equal opportunity, fairness, fair rules, fair markets, level playing field, security, safety

Our vision: *We need a marketplace that is fair to everyone. That requires fundamental rules to ensure consumer products are safe and the terms of sales and investments are open and honest. In four ways, we need to guarantee that everyone plays by the same fair rules by: (1) ensuring that food is safe, drugs are pure, and products are free from dangerous defects; (2) compelling all businesses to follow basic rules of economic decency; (3) protecting individuals' private information; and (4) guaranteeing justice for average Americans and small businesses in civil litigation.*

Conservatives argue against consumer protections on the grounds that such requirements interfere with the *free market*. But American markets are not, and never have been, free of government influence. Governments not only inspect food and drugs, regulate pollution, and impose safety and health standards, they also provide subsidies, contracts, tax breaks, patents and copyrights, protection from imports, and erect barriers to labor organizing.

There is never a question of whether government is involved in markets, the only question is who benefits from the involvement.

That's why progressives favor *fair markets* instead of *free markets*. By fair, we mean markets where governments work to create a level playing field so that individuals and small businesses compete on a reasonably fair basis against the rich and powerful. That is the point of consumer protection. (For more about *fair markets*, see Chapter 19.)

When you fight for laws that protect customers from unfair contract provisions and outright scams, state your arguments in favor of fair rules and level playing fields and against policies that rig the system to benefit the rich.

One type of consumer protection that has been under continuous attack is labeled *tort reform* by conservatives.

Torts and Civil Justice

The system that handles lawsuits among individuals and corporations should be called the *civil justice* system.

Don't say . . .

- Tort reform
- Lawsuit abuse
- Trial lawyer
- Personal injury lawyer

Say . . .

- Civil justice
- Equal justice, justice
- Just and fair compensation
- Hold corporations accountable when they duck responsibility for misconduct
- Rig the system

Why . . .

The right-wing *tort reform* strategy is to focus attention on the victim's lawyer and ignore the victim, the injury, the misconduct and the perpetrator. We must do the opposite: focus on victims, injuries, misconduct and perpetrators, not the attorneys. Americans understand that courts must deliver *justice*, so use that term. And polls show that voters are actually more worried about corporate abuse of consumers, employees and shareholders than abuses by lawyers or plaintiffs.

Make it clear that what our right-wing opponents call tort reform isn't reform at all. It's a cruel shifting of costs from rich companies that caused injuries to the unfortunate people who were injured. And that's unfair. Whenever possible, use local examples to make your case and get the focus back where it should be.

Say . . .

Our courts need to deliver justice. We cannot deny innocent people just and fair compensation for injuries, especially when they're taking on rich and powerful corporations. We need a level playing field. This extreme right wing proposal would rig the system to shift the cost of injuries from a corporation that's at fault to the victim who is innocent. We need policies that uphold equal justice for all.

Why . . .

Why say we cannot deny … just and fair compensation instead of we must ensure they receive just and fair compensation? Persuadable voters are more strongly moved by a plea framed as protecting people from being denied something than one framed as giving or providing that same right.

Don't say . . .	**Say . . .**
• Give rights	• Don't deny rights

Right wing argument: Tort reform saves everyone money by stopping frivolous litigation.

Say . . .

The goal of our legal system is justice. This kind of legislation rigs the system to make it harder for injured Americans to hold wrongdoers accountable. Rich and powerful corporations push for this special treatment because it shifts the responsibility of paying for the cost of injuries from them—the ones who caused the damage—to the innocent victim. That is clearly not justice.

Right wing argument: We need tort reform because medical malpractice lawsuits jack up health care costs.

Say . . .

The inherent purpose of our court system is justice. We should not rig the system to benefit either one side or another. In addition, the Congressional Budget Office found that restricting lawsuits for medical negligence would have virtually no effect on the price we pay for health insurance. At the same time, it would punish innocent victims. That's not justice.

8. EDUCATION

Begin in agreement, for example: We need public schools for our families and our communities that provide each and every child the opportunity to achieve their fullest potential in life.

Our values: Opportunity, equal opportunity, fairness, fair share, opportunity for each and every child

Our vision: *Our public schools must provide each and every child the opportunity to achieve their fullest potential in life. Children are not standardized; each one needs and deserves personalized instruction. That requires both fully qualified professional teachers and opportunities to learn outside of class. Every jurisdiction needs to: (1) provide adequate funding for public schools; (2) deliver instruction in a way that recognizes the differences in both the interests and needs of specific children; (3) provide opportunities to learn outside of classroom time including afterschool, arts and recreational programs, and libraries; and (4) make schools a safe and fair environment for everyone.*

Public education is under attack from conservatives who are, in essence, promoting a corporate takeover of public schools. To push back, you need to understand where voters stand on K-12 education issues.

On standardized testing: Fifty-seven percent of Americans believe "there is too much emphasis on standardized testing in schools." Only 36 percent think there is the right amount or not enough testing. Fifty-five percent oppose linking teacher evaluations to students' standardized test scores. The public is simply not on the testing bandwagon.

On charter schools and vouchers: Forty-four percent favor and 35 percent oppose "the formation of charter schools," a political standoff. Similarly, Americans just marginally favor private school vouchers by a margin of 44 to 39 percent. And yet, Americans think "the focus should be on reforming the existing public school system" (78 percent) "rather than finding an alternative" (22 percent).

On trust in teachers: Sixty percent of Americans rate the honesty and ethical standards of teachers to be high or very high. The only professionals with a higher rating are nurses, doctors and pharmacists. Teachers are substantially more trusted than police, judges and clergy, and are three times more trusted than lawyers, business executives and stockbrokers. Sixty-six percent say teachers are underpaid while only six percent think they are overpaid.

On the quality of schools: When asked to grade schools "A, B, C, D or Fail," only 19 percent say that public schools nationally deserve an A or B. Among the same Americans, 43 percent believe public schools in their own communities deserve an A or B. And among Americans with a child in school, 70 percent would give their school an A or B.

Because Americans like and trust their local schools and teachers, and because voters generally care more about how policies affect their own communities, you should lean heavily on arguments based on how an education policy will impact local schools and schoolchildren.

Say . . .

We need public schools for our families and our communities that provide each and every child the opportunity to reach their fullest potential in life. To accomplish that, we should recognize there are no standardized children; every child has different strengths and weaknesses. That's why our schools must offer a complete curriculum provided by professional teachers who have the training to give the individualized attention every child needs.

Why . . .

The narrative above uses four strategies:

(1) Focus on the listener's own children and neighborhood schools rather than education in the abstract.

(2) Indirectly push back against the overuse of standardized tests and teaching-to-the-test by explicitly pointing out something that every parent knows: every child is different and requires individualized attention.

(3) Change the narrative about school quality measured by average test scores to a narrative about how well our schools provide each and every student the opportunity to learn and excel.

(4) Insist that only professional teachers, rather than amateurs or computer programs, have the knowledge and skills to do the job right.

Don't say . . .

- The nation's schools
- High-poverty schools
- Failing schools, failing teachers
- Soft bigotry of low expectations
- Student achievement

Say . . .

- Our children, local schools, schools in our community
- Opportunity to learn, to succeed
- Teaching-to-the-test, one-size-fits-all
- Each and every child is different, is unique, is an individual
- Professional teacher; teaching profession

Why . . .

The American value behind public education is equal opportunity for all. Instead of addressing the problem that too many children are denied an equal opportunity to learn, the right wing tries to exacerbate it with vouchers, or as they call them, *opportunity scholarships*. Their strategy is to take advantage of the fact that Americans believe public schools outside of their own communities are failing and, instead of fixing them, offer vouchers to enable individual students to escape. The political goal of vouchers is to set some parents against others, particularly within communities of color.

The right wing also appeals to Americans' fervent belief in the market system and urges that parents be treated as consumers and schools be run like corporations. But schools are not businesses, teachers are not factory workers, and students are most certainly not products for sale. After more than a decade of right-wing education policy, there is still no evidence that any of their proposals actually benefit schoolchildren.

The major difference between the partisans on education is that progressives accept responsibility for improving our public schools while conservatives want to abandon them entirely. That's how we should distinguish our positions in public debate. For example, say you are arguing against larger class sizes:

Say . . .

Each and every child in our community deserves the opportunity to grow up to live a successful life. So every child needs excellent schools and professional teachers. Smaller class sizes help children learn because they allow teachers to spend more one-on-one time with each student, providing the individualized instruction they need.

Why . . .

Whatever your progressive solution—whether it's smaller class sizes, modernized school facilities and equipment, programs to attract and retain excellent teachers, a broader and richer curriculum—emphasize the underlying value of equal opportunity and focus on what's best for *each and every child*, which our listeners visualize as their own child or grandchild. If your solution is more resources for public schools, specify how you'd use the money: *for art, music, science labs, technology...what every child needs to succeed.*

Similarly, if you are opposing legislation that would drain resources from local public schools, emphasize that. For example, if you are speaking against spending taxpayer dollars for private school vouchers.

Say . . .

Each and every child in our community deserves access to an excellent neighborhood public school so that child has the opportunity to grow up and be successful in life. There is a proposal to spend your tax dollars on vouchers for private schools, which would mean less money spent on public schools. There is no credible study that shows vouchers improve student performance. So vouchers are neither wise nor fair.

Why . . .

There are lots of statistics about vouchers and you are welcome to use a few. But voters already oppose vouchers if they come at the expense of the public schools, so focus on that.

Finally, don't repeat the anti-teacher and anti-child message frames. They do not support progressive arguments.

Don't say . . .

- School reform, education reform
- Run schools like businesses
- Achievement gap

Say . . .

- Each child deserves an excellent education, personalized instruction
- Opportunity gap

Why . . .

Our nation's future is on the line. Progressives need to re-take the moral high ground on public education. A little smart message framing can make a real difference.

9. ENVIRONMENT & SMART GROWTH

Begin in agreement, for example: We need to protect our community's health and safety, and our quality of life.

Our values: Security, safety, health, protection, quality of life

Our vision: *We have a responsibility to protect the quality of life, not just for ourselves, but for our children and grandchildren. To do that we need to both stop the degradation of our environment now and pursue policies that build a better future. These goals fit into three categories, laws that: (1) reduce the pollution of our air, water and land—including gases that accelerate climate change; (2) conserve energy and quickly develop clean and renewable sources of energy; and (3) pursue policies that build infrastructure to create environmentally friendly cities and towns for the future.*

Since the 2016 election, Americans have been more worried about "the quality of the environment" than they've ever been in this century, and 64 percent think the environment "as a whole is getting worse."

Nevertheless, when you speak to voters, they are mostly concerned about how environmental issues affect them directly. They are worried about their own air quality and local parks, streams and wetlands. So you should personalize your language—it's about the *air we breathe*, the *water we drink*; it's about health and safety *for our children*. Here is a generic message that you can adapt to fit issues in your community:

Say . . .

We've got to protect our community's health and safety, and our quality of life. We understand that includes [keeping our rivers and streams clean. The Big Bend Project would eliminate a great deal of our city's water pollution problem.] This is the time for our [city/county] to take the responsibility to preserve the quality of life in [Big Bend], not just for ourselves, but for our children and grandchildren.

Why . . .

First agree with your audience and explain the progressive values that underlie environmentalism which are all in the *security* column of values: safety, health and quality of life. Make the issue personal by talking about *our* rivers and *our* health, and remind them that any environmental cause benefits their families.

Of course, you need to explain how your specific solution delivers the security that voters seek, and some audiences require more facts than others. Progressives almost always give too many facts upfront and ignore crucial message framing. Focus more on staying in agreement, voicing your values, and helping your audience understand how they benefit.

Don't say . . .

- Opportunity

Say . . .

- Our safety, security, health
- Our quality of life
- For our children and grandchildren

Why . . .

In the environmental debate, the right wing tries to use the value of *opportunity*: the opportunity to mine, drill or develop, for short-term profit. Your job is to move your audience from an opportunity or business/consumer conversation to a discussion about our families' current and long-term security.

For example, let's say you are arguing for restrictions on the drilling technique called hydraulic fracturing, which you should refer to as *fracking*.

Say . . .

We need to guarantee that our drinking water is safe. We need to protect our community's rivers and streams. There is plenty of evidence that fracking can pollute groundwater. Right now, companies engaged in fracking aren't even required to disclose crucial information to scientists so we can know how dangerous it is. We need a fully effective reporting system [or a moratorium] to protect our health and safeguard our quality of life.

Why . . .

Like other environmental issues, base your arguments on the value of security and personalize the issue to your audience.

Anti-environmentalists want to soften the negatives associated with exploiting the environment, so they call drilling and mining *exploring for energy.* Obviously, say *drilling, mining, fracking* and *exploiting* instead.

Don't say . . .

- Exploring for energy

Say . . .

- Drilling for oil/gas
- Fracking
- Exploiting our natural resources

Climate Change

Polling shows that 65 percent of Americans are "very" or "somewhat concerned" about climate change and only six percent believe it "is not occurring."

However, there is an enormous partisan gap on the issue. Fully 71 percent of Republicans believe the threat of climate change is "generally exaggerated" while only 10 percent of Democrats think it's exaggerated. Similarly, 75 percent of Democrats believe that "it has already begun to happen" while only 36 percent of Republicans accept that fact. This is a classic example of confirmation bias, stoked by the right-wing media.

Persuadable Americans' views on climate change are closer to the Democrats than the Republicans. But, like so many issues, the persuadables know very little about the facts. Because only about one-in-ten Americans know that there is a strong scientific consensus on this issue, a Yale study suggests that one fact is especially persuasive: Over 97 percent of climate scientists agree that humans are causing climate change.

Say . . .

We must protect the health, safety and security of our children and grandchildren, and they face a serious problem. Over 97 percent of climate scientists agree that humans are causing climate change. We need to apply commonsense strategies now. We know how to implement clean energy solutions and we know that reducing fossil fuel dependence will make America stronger and our kids safer. It's time to step up and get it done...our children's futures depend on it.

If you're engaged in a longer back-and-forth conversation, you might add: The last five years were the hottest years ever recorded for global temperatures, and 19 of the 20 hottest years on record have occurred since 2000.

Expanding Renewable Energy

At the state and local levels, it is common for progressives to try to enact legislation to expand the percentage of energy generated by renewable sources.

When you're talking about such a policy, avoid the partisan gap over climate change. Use arguments that are more personal, like *we need to reduce air pollution to cut down on respiratory diseases like asthma*, or more generally, promote renewable energy with *we need to work toward a cleaner energy future for [your jurisdiction].*

A prominent conservative polling firm found that Trump voters "support taking action to accelerate the development and use of clean energy" by a margin of 3-to-1 and soft Republicans favor it by 6-to-1. (Democrats support this by 48-to-1.) According to that research:

> When Republicans hear the phrase *clean energy*, they think of solar and wind power. They say it is non-polluting and leads to clean air and renewable energy. There is some concern about the cost and government regulations, but that is outweighed by the positives.

10. GOVERNMENT PERFORMANCE

Begin in agreement, for example: Our laws, rules and programs should be enforced fairly and equally to ensure that everyone gets a fair shot, everyone gives their fair share, and everyone plays by the same rules.

Our values: Opportunity, equal opportunity, justice, fairness, fair share, level playing field

Our vision: *State and local governments play a powerful role as rule-makers and enforcers, and as employers and contractors. A progressive government will: (1) ensure that the workers of both the government and its contractors are paid wages and benefits that support a decent standard of living; (2) guarantee that economic development subsidies are used sparingly and only to create middle-class jobs; and (3) operate with transparency and the highest ethical standards.*

Conservatives have worked very hard to denigrate government, and to some extent they have been successful. Voters are quite cynical about *Washington*. Despite negative stereotypes about the federal government, however, citizens like their state governments and appreciate local governments even more.

Further, even when people say they don't like *government*, they still like what government does. For example, when asked about federal spending programs individually, there's only one program that most Americans would cut: aid to foreign counties. Voters do not want to cut federal spending on health care, environmental protection, energy, scientific research, infrastructure, education or Social Security. And when asked if they have a favorable or unfavorable impression of well-known federal agencies, Americans favor the FDA, OSHA, and the Consumer Product Safety Commission by margins of 2-to-1 or more. The Environmental Protection Agency (EPA), which has been the subject of unrelenting attack by conservatives, is still favored 52-to-33.

In short, when talking about government and its performance, avoid generalities and focus on the benefits of government programs.

Don't say . . .

- Government
- Bureaucracy
- Washington

Say . . .

- Public health and safety
- Roads, schools, parks, libraries
- Consumer protection, environmental protection
- Fair treatment of workers, fair markets, fair trade

Why...

Stay away from *government*, *bureaucracy*, and especially *Washington* to avoid triggering negative stereotypes. And yet, don't hesitate to say *rules, laws*, and even *regulations*.

Lake Research Partners performed two rounds of in-depth public opinion research to probe people's feelings about government rules, regulations, agencies and enforcement. This research found that Americans want more enforcement of rules and regulations, not less. The problem people have with government enforcement is that they feel the rules are not being applied fairly. They think the rich and powerful can get away with whatever they want, that the privileged class can break the rules without consequences.

When asked, "do you think that increased enforcement of our national laws and regulations is a good thing or a bad thing," citizens answered it is a "good thing" by a margin of 71-to-14. State enforcement is even more popular than federal enforcement. More than 2/3rds complain that laws and regulations are not "equally" or "fairly" applied.

These findings do not only apply to enforcement of laws and regulations currently on the books. They can also be used to justify new laws and regulations. Americans don't really know the difference between making laws and regulations stricter and having stricter enforcement of what's on the books. Here's why that's important.

Lake Research gave respondents a choice between two narratives. The conservative narrative was:

> Protecting consumers is important but government regulation has gone too far, so that some politicians seem to think government is the answer to every problem. Increased regulation, bureaucratic red tape, mandates, and uneven enforcement hold back economic growth and

destroy jobs. America was built on the free market and free enterprise. Forcing entrepreneurs, small business owners, and citizens to submit to arbitrary government regulations puts all the power in the hands of out-of-touch bureaucrats. It raises the costs of goods and services at a time when we can't afford higher prices.

That's an excellent description of the conservative message. The progressive narrative went like this:

Say . . .

Proper enforcement of our laws and regulations can ensure that everyone plays by the same set of rules. Today, the system is too often rigged to favor the wealthy and powerful over ordinary Americans, or big corporations over small businesses. That's an argument for better enforcement. Whether prohibiting big banks from destroying our economy, stopping the credit card industry from charging hidden fees, or preventing the wealthiest one percent from hiding billions of tax dollars in offshore tax havens—we need stronger, more just enforcement of our laws and regulations to ensure that everyone has a fair shot.

Given this choice, Americans agreed with the progressive narrative by a margin of 80-to-16. That's a landslide. It means this is a powerful way to frame our arguments. And this progressive narrative promotes policies that could be accomplished by either new regulations or new statutes.

11. HEALTH

Begin in agreement, for example: For decades, our healthcare system has been overpriced and unfair.

Our values: Health, health security, safety, protection, quality of life

Our vision: *Every American should be able to get the health care they need, when they need it, at a price they can afford. But for years, insurance companies charged too much, their policies were full of holes, and coverage was easily denied or revoked. The Affordable Care Act changed that, providing families with a new and greater measure of health security. Now that the ACA is under attack, there is much to be done: (1) guarantee coverage to every American as a matter of right; (2) encourage healthy behavior and protect others from unhealthy behaviors; and (3) allow people to make their own health care choices.*

As the Affordable Care Act (ACA) has come under attack by the Trump Administration, it has become more and more popular. Persuadable voters do not want to lose their health insurance coverage or any guarantee of coverage, pay more in premiums or deductibles, or see a cut in government funding for their health care programs.

The key to persuasion is to focus on what they will or may lose.

Say . . .

For decades, our healthcare system has been overpriced and unfair. Our goal must be to get you—and everyone else—the health care you need, when you need it, at a price you can afford. The [conservative proposal] would hand our healthcare system back to the big insurance companies, allowing them to deny coverage for essential medical care, jack up premiums for women and older Americans, and make insurance completely unaffordable for anyone with a wide range of preexisting conditions. For the security and health of your family and mine, we cannot allow it.

Why . . .

You must personalize the debate. You are welcome to say that millions of Americans will lose health insurance, but don't reference Medicaid. The fact is, few persuadable voters think their own insurance is actually at stake. But it is! Focus on the aspects of the conservative bill that directly or indirectly affect families that get health insurance through an employer. Emphasize over and over that each and every one of their families will likely be harmed if this proposal is enacted. Here's another version.

Say . . .

Protect your own health. Don't let this right-wing legislation put insurance companies back in control of your health care, allowing them to deny you coverage for essential medical care, jack prices way up if you have a preexisting condition, and charge you unfairly high prices if you are in your 50s or 60s, or you're a woman, or simply because you happen to live in an unprofitable state. You must understand: the right-wing plan will devastate health care for everyone, including people who get insurance through their jobs.

Why . . .

As we emphasize throughout this book, persuadable voters want to know how the policy affects themselves, their families, and their friends. Tell them!

Don't say . . .

- Them
- The poor, people in poverty
- Give health insurance

Say . . .

- You and your family
- Hardworking Americans
- Families, children, people with disabilities
- Don't deny the security of health care

Why . . .

When the conversation turns to the uninsured, avoid language about poverty because it evokes negative ideas about welfare. Use the terms *hard-working, families, children*, and *people with disabilities* because these suggest the recipients need and deserve basic medical coverage. And as we have explained elsewhere, it's more effective to say *don't deny them the security* instead of *give them the security.*

Use similar tactics for proactive progressive legislation designed to strengthen the healthcare system. For example:

Say . . .

For decades, our healthcare system has been overpriced and unfair. Our goal must be to get you—and everyone else—the health care you need, when you need it, at a price you can afford. One crucial step is to minimize uncompensated care. That's when uninsured people get healthcare in the most expensive way, at hospital emergency rooms, and then that cost is added onto our insurance premiums. Getting them covered saves you money.

Prescription drugs

Until the Trump Administration started attacking the Affordable Care Act, Americans said their top health care policy priority was to lower prescription drug prices, especially high-cost drugs for chronic conditions like HIV, hepatitis, mental illness and cancer. In fact, 90 percent of Americans believe it is an "important" or "top priority" to pass "legislation to bring down the price of prescription drugs."

Say . . .

Prescription drug prices are skyrocketing. To protect our health, all of our families need access to medicines that are affordable. No one should ever have to choose between buying medicine or paying their rent. A new proposal in our state legislature would [create a Prescription Drug Affordability Board to ensure that drug costs aren't unfairly high]. The bill helps all of us, and for someone you know, it may actually be a matter of life and death.

Why . . .

You are welcome to cite facts and figures, and there are a lot of them on this topic. But average Americans are already convinced of the need, you just have to connect their preexisting beliefs about prescription drug prices to specific legislation that requires their support.

Tobacco

Tobacco products such as cigarettes, cigars and chewing tobacco are the leading cause of preventable death in the United States despite decades of public education. And, in reaction to smoking regulations, the tobacco industry is producing and promoting new e-cigarette products that come in flavors that are attractive to young people. The public health consequences of tobacco disproportionately affect low-income Americans, communities of color, and people in the military—all of whom have long been proactively targeted by the industry.

Don't say . . .

- Smokers' freedom
- Smokers' rights

Say . . .

- Smoke-free, secondhand smoke
- Protect everyone's health, prevent diseases such as cancer
- Protect the environment
- Protect children, protect nonsmokers
- Expand opportunities for people to quit smoking (or vaping)

Why . . .

Even people who smoke don't believe anyone has the freedom or right to hurt others. In fact, the majority of people who smoke want to try to quit. On the state and local levels, most of the debate revolves around two health policies. First, smoke-free workplaces:

Say . . .

We have a responsibility to protect the public health, especially when it comes to children. Years of research have clearly shown that secondhand smoke is dangerous and cancerous. Doctors and scientists have concluded that the only way to protect nonsmokers from secondhand smoke is to require smoke-free workplaces. That's what we should do to defend everyone's right to breathe clean air.

Why . . .

Americans overwhelmingly believe that secondhand smoke is harmful. They are concerned about their own health, and it is persuasive to talk about children's health. Less than 20 percent of voters smoke and even a good percentage of them support smoke-free laws.

The other common smoking/vaping-related political debate is about raising the tax on these products.

Say . . .

As adults, we have a responsibility to protect children from harm. Sadly, one-third of kids who smoke cigarettes will die prematurely from smoking-related illnesses. And the nicotine in e-cigarettes is both addictive and dangerous. The most proven, effective way to protect our children is to raise the taxes on these products. When the tax goes up, teen smoking goes down. It's a small price to pay to protect the health of our children.

Why . . .

For voters, deemphasize tax revenues and focus on health benefits. Legislators are interested in what they can do with the tax dollars but that's not a strong argument to persuadable voters.

Right wing argument: Secondhand smoke is not a health hazard.

Say . . .

We need to protect our health. The Centers for Disease Control, the U.S. Surgeon General, and all the other important health organizations unanimously agree that smoke is just as dangerous to another person exposed to it as it is to the smoker. Children are the ones most often affected. The American Lung Association estimates that, in the U.S., secondhand smoke causes more than 40,000 deaths per year.

Right wing argument: Anti-tobacco laws infringe on a person's right to smoke.

Say . . .

I feel for smokers; tobacco is extremely addictive and expensive. I would certainly support programs to help them stop smoking. We should also make sure everyone has the right to breathe clean air and not have their own health damaged. These laws do not stop anyone from smoking; they simply stop some of the harms that smoking inflicts on others.

12. PUBLIC SAFETY

Begin in agreement, for example: The most basic job of our city/county/state is to keep you safe from crime.

Our values: Security, safety, protection, justice

Our vision: *The most fundamental job of government is to protect its citizens from crime. Progressive government focuses on strategies that make us safer and serious felonies deserve serious punishment. But there is a great deal that can be done to prevent crime while also ensuring justice: (1) reform police procedures, including interrogations and use of force, that lead authorities toward the wrong suspects; (2) reform judicial procedures that hurt the innocent, thereby helping the guilty; (3) reform prison procedures that increase recidivism; and (4) reform criminal laws to prevent the commission of crimes.*

When you're talking about crime, you must tell voters how your policies will make them safer, not how they benefit the perpetrator or suspect.

Don't say . . .

- Rights (of criminals)

Say . . .

- Security, safety, protection
- Responsibility
- Justice

Why . . .

Do not begin a discussion of crime with the ideas of fairness or equal opportunity. Persuadable voters want to know how your criminal justice policies will *protect* them. It shouldn't be hard to explain since that's what all good progressive criminal justice policies accomplish—they prevent crime, reduce recidivism and improve the quality of life for everyone in the community.

Conversely, right wing policies—like giving long prison sentences to non-violent drug offenders—take hundreds of millions of dollars away from strategies that more effectively fight drug abuse and prevent crime.

Say . . .

The most fundamental job of government is to protect you from crime, to make all law-abiding people safer. That means more than punishment. It means diverting nonviolent and young offenders from future crimes. It means changing police procedures that lead authorities toward the wrong suspects. And it means using the best technology to protect the innocent while identifying the guilty. These policies make you and your families safer.

Why . . .

Everyone wants safer communities. But what if the progressive policy is specifically about the rights of the accused? For example, policies to require electronic recording of interrogations, reform police procedures for lineups, and create commissions to research whether imprisoned people are actually innocent.

Emphasize that for every wrongly convicted person there is an actual perpetrator who has escaped justice and remains a threat to our public safety. Point out that there are more modern practices that have been proven to work better than current police procedures. Say that we owe it to the victim, as well as the whole community, to find and punish the real criminal. For example:

Say . . .

The whole point of this legislation is to protect you from crime. A lot of other jurisdictions get better evidence from suspects and witnesses by requiring that all police questioning be electronically recorded. It protects the innocent and makes it easier to convict the guilty. Technology has changed rapidly, and we should take advantage of it.

Gun Violence

Persuadable Americans know almost nothing about gun laws and have no idea how easy it is for dangerous people to buy firearms. When asked about gun policies, they overwhelmingly support background checks and other modest gun laws. (Many think such policies have always been the law.)

Pro-gun advocates know that they lose the argument on the merits, so their tactic is to sidetrack the discussion. Prepare to spend most of your time trying to steer the conversation back to the specific proposal at hand.

Don't say . . .

- Gun control
- Stricter gun laws
- You oppose the 2nd Amendment

Say . . .

- Prevent gun violence
- Stronger gun laws
- Support for the 2nd Amendment goes hand-in-hand with keeping guns out of the hands of dangerous people

Why . . .

The National Rifle Association (NRA) has done an effective job of making people associate the words *gun control* or even *stricter* laws with confiscating guns or banning handguns entirely. Of course, no one is proposing that. You need to make it clear that you are advocating for policies that voters consider reasonable and even modest. Like them, you support the 2nd Amendment. Like them, you don't have a problem with NRA members in your community. (If the situation requires you to attack the NRA, then condemn *NRA lobbyists* or the *NRA's out-of-touch leaders*. Never attack average NRA members or local NRA leaders; that doesn't work.)

To introduce your argument, start with the fundamentals:

Say . . .

We need to do everything we can to keep our community safe and secure from violence. But every day, far too many of us are victims of gun violence. Dozens of Americans *will* be murdered, hundreds of others *will* be shot, and about one thousand *will* be robbed or assaulted with a gun...*today.* (If you can, tell a personal story here.)

Why . . .

Don't skip the universally shared values we are fighting for: *safety* and *security*. And then, don't ignore the fundamental facts that motivate us: there are more than 10,000 gun murders, 100,000 people shot, and 400,000 Americans robbed or assaulted with firearms, every single year. Let people recognize that every day, wherever we go in America, we are all at risk of gun violence. And then:

Say . . .

It is obvious why so many people are killed or victimized with guns, day after day: we have some of the weakest gun laws in the world. To make us, our families and our communities safer, we need to change a few of those laws…now.

Why . . .

Don't assume people understand why we need new laws. Link the problem to the solution. If you're debating background checks for all gun sales, this is your basic argument:

Say . . .

Our community can't be safe if we allow guns to be sold to felons or the dangerously mentally ill. That's why current law requires that no gun can be sold by a *licensed gun dealer* without a criminal background check. But millions of guns are sold by *unlicensed* sellers at gun shows and through Internet sites with no background check. We need a simple change in the law in order to cover all gun sales. The few minutes it takes to complete a computerized check will save lives. It's just common sense.

Why . . .

Since 1968, federal law has banned the possession of firearms by convicted felons, domestic abusers and people who are dangerously mentally ill. The Brady Law, enacted in 1993, requires a criminal background check before any licensed dealer can sell any firearm. (Some states require more.) A National Instant Criminal Background Check System (NICS) for gun purchases, operated by the FBI, began in 1998. Poll after poll shows that Americans overwhelmingly support background checks for all gun sales.

The only direct argument against background checks by the pro-gun lobby is that *criminals will get guns anyway.*

Say . . .

The federal background check law has blocked millions of illegal gun sales. It works. The problem is that the law doesn't apply to private sales, so felons can currently avoid a background check and get any kind of gun, no questions asked. It's time to close the private sales loophole.

Why . . .

Nobody suggests this law will stop all criminals. To be successful, it doesn't have to. No law stops all crime. It's simply common sense to block as many illegal sales as possible. All the other arguments raised in this debate are designed to change the subject. Here are some examples:

Right wing argument: The Second Amendment forbids the proposed gun law.

Say . . .

I support the 2nd Amendment. In fact, the Supreme Court ruled that reasonable gun laws are constitutional, and other federal and state courts have consistently held that a measure on guns like the one we're talking about does not violate the 2nd Amendment. Let's return to the real issue. It is just plain common sense to require background checks for all gun purchases.

Why . . .

The 2008 Supreme Court opinion in *District of Columbia v. Heller* guarantees Americans the right to have a handgun in the home for self-protection. The Court also said: "[N]othing in our opinion should be taken to cast doubt on longstanding prohibitions on the possession of firearms by felons and the mentally ill, or laws forbidding the carrying of firearms in sensitive places such as schools and government buildings, or laws imposing conditions and qualifications on the commercial sale of arms." And that ruling explicitly reaffirmed the Supreme Court's 1939 *U.S. v. Miller* opinion that upheld a law banning sawed-off shotguns (the same law bans machine guns, silencers and grenades) and stated that policymakers have the power to prohibit "dangerous and unusual weapons."

Right wing argument: The assault weapon law wouldn't have stopped a particular massacre, or other claims that a proposed gun law wouldn't have prevented a particular crime.

Say . . .

The goal of public safety legislation is to protect citizens, but no law is 100 percent effective. The law against murder doesn't stop all murders. The law that lowered the blood alcohol level for driving didn't stop all drunk driving. This policy will not stop every gun crime, but it will save some lives. Let's talk about that.

Right wing argument: This law will give the federal government the data to create a gun registration list, and that'll lead to us getting our guns taken away.

Say . . .

The goal of this legislation is to protect citizens, and it will do that. There is nothing in the background check proposal that creates a registry. In fact, existing law forbids the federal government from establishing a gun registration list. Let's return to the real issue. This legislation would require background checks for all gun purchases and that's just simple common sense.

Right wing argument: We should provide armed guards/do something about mental health/make parents take responsibility/ban violent video games instead.

Say . . .

We should make our communities safer. If you've got a good proposal, that's fine. But this is not an either-or debate; one policy does not exclude another. Can we get back to the legislation on the table: why should we sell these guns to any adult, without any background check, no questions asked?

Right wing argument: The only way to stop a bad guy with a gun is a good guy with a gun.

Say . . .

We want a public policy that makes our communities safer. Unfortunately, your "good guy with a gun" story doesn't work in real life. Both Marjory Stoneman Douglas High School and Columbine High School had armed deputy sheriffs on duty when all those children were murdered. Virginia Tech had an entire police force, including a SWAT team. There were several armed police officers at the Las Vegas massacre. The Fort Hood massacre happened at a military base filled with soldiers. President Reagan and his press secretary Jim Brady were surrounded by armed police and Secret Service, and yet both were shot. Let's get back to the real debate over this legislation.

13. REPRODUCTIVE RIGHTS

Begin in agreement, for example: The decision about whether or when to become a parent is a deeply personal and private matter.

Our values: Freedom, liberty, privacy, dignity, respect, personal responsibility

Our vision: *Decisions about contraception and abortion should be made by the individuals involved, not by politicians or the government. To make these decisions responsibly, people need access to: (1) complete and medically accurate information; (2) birth control; (3) constitutionally protected abortion services; and (4) protection from discrimination based on a person's decision to take contraception, give birth, or have an abortion.*

A strong majority of Americans favor keeping abortion legal and oppose overturning *Roe v. Wade*, the 1973 Supreme Court decision that legalized abortion. At the same time, Americans often hold conflicting feelings about abortion and struggle to resolve the conflict. When it comes to public policy, this means that while support for legality remains strong, it is often easy to get the public to favor restrictions on a woman's right to have an abortion, such as waiting periods, sonograms, burdensome rules for abortion clinics, parental consent laws, insurance bans, and more.

The Public Leadership Institute commissioned Ann Selzer to conduct an in-depth nationwide poll on reproductive rights. That research found that several abortion rights narratives work quite well, but especially this:

Say . . .

We cannot know all the personal and medical circumstances behind someone's decision to have an abortion. Every person's situation is different. [Tell a story, if possible.] So, we should respect that this decision is hers to make, with her family and in accordance with her faith.
And once someone has made this very personal and private decision, politicians should not interfere.

Why . . .

By reminding people that they don't know a woman's circumstances, it tends to dispel negative stereotypes that your listeners may hold about women choosing abortion. It increases empathy and decreases a rush to judgment.

In addition, some conflicting feelings are resolved when people focus on what a person's experience should be *after* she has made the decision to have an abortion, rather than *on* her decision. Once a person has made the decision to have an abortion, a strong majority want her experience to be positive—that is, non-judgmental, informed by medically-accurate information, supportive, affordable and without pressure or added burdens.

This is another simple, effective statement:

Say . . .

I appreciate that abortion is a complex issue for the individuals involved. That's why I feel that politicians should stay out of the very personal and private decision whether or not to have an abortion.

Why . . .

Choose the argument that feels right to you. Elected officials and candidates for office may feel that this second version fits best. Note that the first sentence puts you in agreement with persuadable voters by recognizing that they hold conflicting feelings about abortion.

There is another popular way to voice support for abortion rights, but it's not quite the same as the more generic statements above.

Say . . .

I support the constitutional right to an abortion declared by the U.S. Supreme Court more than 45 years ago in the case of *Roe v. Wade.*

Why . . .

More than three-quarters of Americans want to uphold *Roe v. Wade*, so the narrative above is usually the most popular. With a hostile Supreme Court, citing *Roe* may also be the most relevant. However, because the courts have upheld a variety of abortion restrictions despite *Roe*, it's a less sweeping statement of support for the abortion rights movement.

Generally, when talking about reproductive rights:

Don't say . . .

- They, them
- Women, all women, families
- Choice, pro-choice
- Pro-life
- Right
- Listing details or reasons why a woman is having an abortion (e.g., rape, incest, fetal anomalies, etc.)
- Abortion should be safe, legal and rare
- Using the terms fair, unfair, or discriminatory

Say . . .

- We, us
- A woman, a person, her family
- Personal decision, important life decision
- Anti-abortion, abortion opponents
- Ability, should be able to, need
- Mention her decision-making process: "thinking through her decision," "talking it over with loved ones"
- Legal abortion must be available and affordable
- We shouldn't treat people differently just because... (they receive their insurance through Medicaid, live in a certain zip code)

Why . . .

Personalize the conversation. Don't let this be about an abstraction; it's an issue that affects millions of individuals. Unfortunately, the *choice* frame, which worked for many years, now triggers confirmation bias. So, while *pro-choice* remains popular with our base, it won't help you persuade.

Right wing argument: Abortion is immoral/against my beliefs/not what God wants.

Say . . .

Each of us has strong feelings about abortion. Even if we disagree, it's not my place to make a decision for someone else. It is better that each person be able to make her own decision.

Right wing argument: Too many women use abortion as birth control.

Say . . .

In my own experience, I know women weigh their decision carefully, think it through with their family and loved ones, and rely on their spiritual beliefs. We don't know every woman's circumstances. We aren't in her shoes. I don't want to make such an important decision for anyone else, that's not my place.

Right wing argument: Abortion hurts women.

Say . . .

Most important decisions in life trigger complex and conflicting emotions, and abortion is no exception. Some kind of reaction to serious life decisions is normal. Strong feelings are certainly not a reason to take away every person's ability to make important life decisions based on her own unique circumstances.

Right wing argument: Taxpayers shouldn't have to foot the bill for abortion.

Say . . .

However we feel about abortion, politicians shouldn't deny a woman's health coverage for it based simply on her inability to pay.

14. SOCIAL SERVICES

Begin in agreement, for example: We have a responsibility to protect innocent children in our communities.

Our values: Security, safety, protection, quality of life, responsibility

Our vision: *As a society, we have a responsibility to protect people in our communities who are vulnerable and can't meet basic needs on their own. Whether they are children, the elderly, disabled, or victims of illness, crime, natural disaster or something else, we cannot deny our fellow citizens the basic necessities of life. Three policies are crucial: (1) expand basic services to cover all the vulnerable people who need them; (2) stop the war on drug users that has cut them off from assistance; and (3) help charities that provide important social services, including food, housing, clothing, job training and legal representation.*

Progressive policies often involve the delivery of social services. They require the active participation of government as a protector, manager or referee. You need Americans to accept government in those roles, but it can be a challenge. Progressives must navigate a minefield of negative stereotypes and preconceptions.

When you describe progressive social policies, what's the best way to talk about government services? The short answer is to avoid the processes of government and focus on the benefits.

Don't say . . .

- Government
- Bureaucracy
- Washington

Say . . .

- Public health and safety
- Security
- Protection

Why . . .

Persuadable voters don't like government in the abstract. The words *government* and *bureaucracy* bring to mind scenes of unfairness, inefficiency and frustration, so don't provoke those negative associations. Similarly, don't call the federal government *Washington* unless you intend to invoke a powerful negative reaction.

Voters, however, like the results of government—public health and safety, public amenities, and a powerful entity mediating disputes and protecting residents from harm. So when you can, focus on the ends of government and avoid the means.

In fact, avoid saying *government* altogether.

Don't say . . .	Say . . .
• Government	• Community, Society • America • We

Why . . .

When voters hear the word *government,* they may think of stereotypical examples of frustration: the surly health inspector, the incompetent tax help line, or the slow-as-molasses Department of Motor Vehicles.

Instead of government, talk about how *we, our community,* or *our society* should protect children, the elderly, the disabled, or hardworking families that can't make ends meet. Government may not always be popular, but *we* are. People will understand what you're saying.

When you're talking about basic social services:

Don't say . . .	Say . . .
• Welfare • Social services • Safety net • Entitlements	• Basic needs, basic living standards • Necessities • Assistance, support • Can't make ends meet

Why . . .

As you surely know, there is a strong stigma attached to the word welfare; don't use the term. The stigma is connected to the idea that recipients of government assistance are lazy and/or cheaters. Whenever possible, avoid phrases like *social services* and *safety net* and instead talk about *basics* or *necessities*.

Even more important than the way you describe a social services program is how you describe the people who receive services.

Don't say . . .

- Beneficiaries
- The poor, people in poverty
- Welfare recipients
- Seniors

Say . . .

- People in need of temporary assistance
- Children, people with disabilities, the vulnerable
- Working families, working to provide for their families
- Elderly

Why . . .

Outside of the progressive base, it is difficult to convince Americans to support a policy that appears to benefit people other than themselves, their families and their friends. So whenever possible, show voters that they personally benefit from your policy, even when that benefit is indirect. Argue that the policy is for *us*, not *them*.

When you can't avoid talking about aiding other people, make sure to describe them as deserving. You can explain they are the vulnerable in society—such as children, the elderly, and people with disabilities—some of whom need assistance. When the recipients are adults, say that they are *hardworking* or *want to work*. And because the programs you support undoubtedly benefit them, freely use the word *families*. We are pro-family, the radical right is not.

And as mentioned previously, persuadable voters are more strongly moved by a plea framed as protecting people from being *denied* needs, necessities or protections than one framed as *giving* the exact same public service, especially when it's called a right or benefit.

Don't say . . .

- Give rights or benefits

Say . . .

- Don't deny necessities or protections

In sum, talk about social services like this:

Say . . .

The United States is a great and powerful nation. That means, in part, that we have the responsibility to protect people in need, including children, the elderly, the disabled, and the victims of natural disaster or crime. But also, it means we need laws and programs that support every American who works hard and plays by the rules. This strengthens our economy and our society. It makes a better community for all of us.

15. TAXATION

Begin in agreement, for example: Not everyone pays their fair share in taxes, especially the rich.

Our values: Fairness, fair share, justice, equal opportunity, level playing field

Our vision: *On the federal, state and local levels, our tax policies must be fair to everyone. The fact is, our tax system is thoroughly unfair; it is rigged with loopholes and giveaways that benefit only a few, usually rich individuals and big corporations, at the expense of all the rest of us. Everyone should pay their fair share, and to accomplish that, we must: (1) require disclosure of tax giveaways; (2) eliminate those giveaways that unfairly benefit the rich and powerful; (3) raise tax rates on the rich; and (4) cut taxes for people who cannot reasonably afford to pay them.*

Voters are pretty cynical about taxes. About half believe that both lower- and middle-income Americans pay too much in federal taxes. That can be a problem if they think you are trying to raise their taxes.

At the same time, by more than a 3-to-1 margin they believe that upper-income people and corporations are paying too little, and favor increasing taxes on wealthy Americans and large corporations.

Americans think that taxes are unfair, and you certainly agree that tax laws have been engineered to unfairly benefit the rich and special interests. So don't defend taxes, defend tax fairness.

Don't say . . .

- Tax relief
- Taxes are a necessary evil

Say . . .

- Tax fairness
- Tax giveaways and tax loopholes
- Private tax subsidies
- Rigged tax system

Why . . .

Don't say *tax relief* because it frames taxes as an affliction in need of a remedy. The problem is not the existence of taxes, it is that federal, state, and local taxes are riddled with giveaways and loopholes for the politically powerful. You can also call them *private tax subsidies*. Whatever you do, don't defend the unpopular tax system. And don't begin with a raft of statistics either. Start by agreeing with voters.

Say . . .

Our tax system is unfair. The tax burden on working families has increased while rich people and huge corporations have been given tax giveaways and loopholes. That's wrong—everyone should pay their fair share. We need to change the rules to create a tax system that works for all of us, not just the wealthy few. One step is [describe your specific proposal]...

Why . . .

No one likes to pay taxes, and persuadable voters don't want to hear a lecture that taxes are the dues we pay for a civilized society. But people generally accept that they should pay their fair share.

Interestingly, a progressive monologue about taxes becomes less popular if it begins with unfairness and then goes on to say what government could do with the money. This is because persuadable voters don't really believe the government needs more money; they believe one-third to one-half of tax dollars are wasted. Talking about the good things government can do with the taxes it collects also evokes voters' biases against tax-and-spend politicians. So stick with your plea that the powerful need to pay their fair share.

Here are a couple of assertions you may have to deal with:

Right wing argument: Forty-seven percent of Americans pay no taxes.

Say . . .

Everyone needs to pay their fair share of taxes. And in fact, everyone who earns a salary pays taxes for Social Security and Medicare. Everyone who buys products at a store or owns a home pays taxes. Everyone who has a telephone or cable service pays taxes. When all the federal, state and local taxes and fees are added together, almost everybody pays about 20 to 30 percent of their income. But the fact is, the richest individuals and largest companies in America do not pay anywhere near their fair share in taxes.

Right wing argument: We're all hurt by the "death tax."

Say . . .

Everyone should pay their fair share of taxes. If we repealed the tax on inheritance, the system would be far more tilted to benefit the rich. That's because you and I don't pay any inheritance tax, it only applies to the very wealthiest people. They already have more than their fair share of tax breaks. And worse, if we eliminated that source of taxes to the government, you and I would have to make up the difference. If you're for tax fairness, you're for keeping the inheritance tax.

16. VOTING & ELECTIONS

Begin in agreement, for example: In a democracy, the right to vote is a fundamental freedom.

Our values: Freedom, liberty, fundamental rights, basic rights, democracy

Our vision: *In America, the right to vote is a fundamental freedom. And because we are the leading democracy in the world, our election system ought to be completely free, fair and accessible. The way we conduct elections today is obsolete. We need to eliminate long lines, cut costs, make it more convenient for eligible citizens to vote, maintain the integrity of the voting system, and stop the rich and powerful from exercising undue influence on the process. In short, we must: (1) guarantee that every citizen can register to vote; (2) ensure that all citizens can cast their ballots; and (3) crack down on the way campaign financing corrupts public policy.*

In general, progressives seek to make voter registration simpler and more accurate and voting more convenient. Right wingers try to make it harder for eligible Americans to register and vote. Your argument is based on freedom, patriotism and the modernization of our outmoded voting systems. Their argument is based on the unfounded fear of voter fraud, often imagined as fraudulent voting by African Americans and immigrants.

Whether you are arguing for a progressive reform or against a right-wing restriction, begin with a statement of your values.

Say . . .

In America, the right to vote is a fundamental freedom. And because we are the leading democracy in the world, our election system ought to be completely free, fair and accessible.

Why . . .

You must put the conversation in context. When talking about voting, progressives have two great advantages that are too-rarely used by our side:

First, the most popular and powerful value in political debate is *freedom*. Use it here. If voting is understood as a basic right like freedom of speech, then it should never be curbed unless it risks an immediate, serious threat to public security (shouting fire in a crowded theater). Our freedom to vote should never be limited without an overriding reason, and none exists. If you can win the frame that voting is a fundamental freedom, you'll ultimately win the argument.

Second, Americans are proud of American democracy and an appeal to that feeling of patriotism helps to persuade them.

Here's a narrative that opposes voting restrictions generally:

Say . . .

In America, the right to vote is a fundamental freedom. And because we are the leading democracy in the world, our election system must be free, fair and accessible for every qualified voter. As we protect election integrity, we cannot infringe on freedom. When the government puts up barriers, it creates long lines for everyone, increases taxpayer costs, and denies the vote to millions of senior citizens and military veterans. Let's stick to efficient and effective ways to keep our elections honest.

What to say about voter fraud

If someone tries to cast a ballot by impersonating an eligible voter, that's a crime punishable by years in prison. Because the penalty is severe, with no real advantage to the perpetrator, this crime almost never happens. And yet, impersonation is the only kind of voter fraud that could be prevented by requiring people to display photo identification.

The problem is, many Americans firmly believe that voter fraud exists. According to a Washington Post/ABC News poll, 46 percent of all voters and 69 percent of Trump voters believe that very or somewhat often "the same person vot[es] multiple times or someone vote[s] who is not eligible." Americans probably believe that because we do have an anecdotal history of "voting from the graveyard," and the 2000 election exposed the fact that some election administrators are extremely inept.

Don't say . . .

- Voter fraud
- Illegal voting
- Voter suppression or disenfranchisement

Say . . .

- Fundamental freedom
- Most basic right in a democracy
- Free, fair and accessible
- Making it harder to vote

Why . . .

Expect the right wing to cry *voter fraud* no matter what legislation is being considered. The best messaging advice is—don't say the F-word. You cannot win the argument by educating voters that fraud is rare. Instead, acknowledge the importance of protecting the integrity of our elections and push the debate away from fraud and toward the goal of making elections *free, fair and accessible.* That poll-tested phrase is discussed in the report *How to Talk About Voting* from the Brennan Center for Justice and the Advancement Project. It works. And don't use the language *voter suppression* or *disenfranchisement* because those are polarizing terms; say "making it harder to vote" or "making it harder to exercise our freedom to vote" instead.

When arguing against voter ID legislation, appeal to freedom and patriotism as suggested in the narrative above, and then:

Say . . .

Protecting the integrity of our elections is absolutely essential. In the process, we cannot infringe on freedom; we cannot deny voters an election that is free, fair and accessible. If we require Election Day precinct officials to scrutinize each and every voter's identification and limit the types of qualified ID to just a few, it will create long lines for everyone, increase election costs by millions of dollars, and make it much harder for Americans who don't have a driver's license—including senior citizens and military veterans—to vote in our democracy. There are more effective ways to keep our elections honest without making it harder for all of us to exercise our fundamental freedom to vote.

Why . . .

The narrative above never uses the word fraud and does not dispute the existence of voter fraud. It suggests instead that this particular legislation is flawed. Specifically, it makes three points:

1. *Long lines*—In considering any policy, people first want to know how it affects them personally. Voter ID will increase everyone's waiting time at the polls, perhaps by a lot. Let voters understand they will be personally inconvenienced by this law.

2. *Taxpayer costs*—Right now any unnecessary government spending is unpopular. A photo ID requirement means the government will have

to pay to educate voters about the new rules, educate precinct officials, and perhaps pay for staff or machinery in order to speed up the delays it will cause. This may sound like a small point, but it played a big role in winning the Minnesota referendum on voter ID.

3. *Making it harder to vote*—This is the most important argument but, to be effective, limit your examples to the most sympathetic victims. Average Americans can be persuaded by focusing on seniors and veterans who are lifelong voters; often they no longer have valid driver's licenses and they would have a hard time getting substitute ID. Swing voters are less likely to be persuaded by hearing about people in poverty who lack identification.

Do not underestimate the difficulty of the progressive argument. Average Americans generally believe the conservative talking points are true. After all, they have to show photo ID whenever they get on an airplane and even when they buy Sudafed at the drugstore. Why not require it to vote? Understand that you start this debate at a severe disadvantage, so you must be mindful of Americans' beliefs and use the best-informed messaging to win them over.

Progressive voting reforms

In many states, the voter registration and Election Day systems are ancient, inefficient and inaccurate. That's why we need to modernize these systems with processes and technologies that are commonplace everywhere else except in the administration of elections.

Say . . .

We need to uphold the freedom to vote for every eligible American citizen. One important step is to modernize the election process with [online registration/early voting/automatic transfer/another reform]. This will benefit all of us by eliminating long lines at the polls, cutting administrative costs, making it more convenient for eligible citizens to vote, and maintaining the integrity of the voting system. It will help make our elections free, fair and accessible for every one of us.

Why . . .

Progressives usually want to talk about how automatic, online or Election Day registration helps people who are not registered. They want to explain how early or absentee voting helps people who aren't otherwise able to vote. But overwhelmingly, the audience you're trying to persuade is registered and manages to vote. So you need to talk about how progressive reforms benefit them personally—for example, how listeners deserve the convenience of their voter registration being automatically transferred to a new address when they move.

There are many important proactive election reforms. When you argue for any of them, appeal to modern technologies and modern life. "The system needs to be modernized and brought into the 21st century." "Today's outdated system is vulnerable to manipulation and human error." "In this day and age, no one should ever be denied the fundamental freedom to vote when commonplace technology can ensure our elections are free, fair and accessible."

Right wing argument: Online registration will lead to voter fraud.

Say . . .

We need to ensure that our elections are free, fair and accessible for everyone who is eligible to vote. Most states now use online voter registration because it saves money, reduces errors, and speeds up the line to vote on Election Day. Those states have proven that online registration actually leads to more accurate voter rolls, not more mistakes. It's time to replace our outmoded and inaccurate voting systems with modern technology.

Right wing argument: Early voting is not worth the cost.

Say . . .

Our elections should be free, fair and accessible for every eligible voter. Restricting the vote to one particular Tuesday is inconsistent with the requirements of modern life. That's why most states now allow citizens to vote before Election Day or vote absentee. This increases convenience, and at the same time, diminishes the number of people who vote on Election Day which eliminates long lines at the polls. The fact is, it costs very little to replace our ancient and inefficient policy of Election Day voting with a modern system that benefits everyone.

17. WAGES & BENEFITS

Begin in agreement, for example: America should be a land of opportunity, where hard work is rewarded.

Our values: Opportunity, equal opportunity, fairness, fair share, justice, level playing field

Our vision: *Our economic system is unfair because the rules are rigged to favor the rich and powerful over the middle class and working families. We need to ensure that lower-level jobs provide at least a living wage and that middle-class jobs support a middle-class standard of living. Four policies are fundamental, laws that: (1) set a floor on wages for different types of work; (2) guarantee a minimum set of job benefits; (3) ensure that hiring and retention processes are fair; and (4) protect the right to collective bargaining in order to secure for workers a fair share of the profits.*

Progressives have often focused on legislation to create jobs, and that's a worthy goal, of course. But in today's economy, voters are much more interested in policies that provide better wages and benefits. A CBS News/New York Times poll, for example, found that more than 70 percent of Americans favor a substantial increase in the minimum wage, 80 percent favor paid leave for parents to take care of newborn children and sick family members, and 85 percent favor paid sick leave for employees when they are ill.

So, audiences are prepared to agree with progressive narratives about improving wages and benefits. For example:

Say . . .

For too many hardworking Americans, wages and benefits haven't kept up with the cost of living. And because it is middle class and working families who drive our economy, the lack of decent wages and benefits hurts everyone. Therefore, we must rewrite some economic rules so that workers get a fair deal by [specific legislation]. This policy helps build an economy that works for everyone, not just the wealthy few.

Why . . .

Every message about wages and benefits should explicitly say the beneficiaries are hard working. Use the values associated with equal opportunity, such as *fairness*, *fair share*, *fair deal*, and *level playing field*. And again, explicitly point a finger at the rich and powerful.

Minimum Wage

The federal minimum wage is only $7.25 an hour. More than 70 percent of voters support raising it to $10 an hour, around 60 percent support $12 an hour, and a majority would raise it to $15 an hour. This cause is both great politics and great policy; every progressive should embrace the issue.

Generally, persuadable voters earn more than the minimum wage. So you need to show them that they indirectly benefit from an increase in the minimum wage and that the people receiving direct benefits are deserving.

Say . . .

America must be a land of opportunity, where hard work is rewarded. But today's minimum wage is not enough for a family to make ends meet. Raising the minimum wage puts money in the pockets of hardworking Americans who will spend it on the things they need. This, in turn, generates business for our economy and eases the burden on taxpayer-funded services. It's a win-win. Raising the minimum wage helps build an economy that works for everyone, not just the rich.

Why . . .

Many progressive advocates want to start with facts and figures. Please don't. Most Americans are already on your side so take this opportunity to show how the policy they already understand and favor is based on your progressive values.

Here are the key arguments to make. An increased minimum wage:

- *Rewards work*—raising the minimum wage shows that we value hard work and people who work hard;
- *Boosts the economy*—the public already believes this, so say it loudly;
- *Saves taxpayer money*—if families make a decent wage, it reduces their need for government programs; and

- *Promotes fairness*—people remain quite angry about CEO pay and the unfairness that pervades today's economy; workers deserve their fair share.

There is also language to avoid. Don't make the minimum wage about alleviating poverty. The reality is that persuadable voters will default to negative stereotypes they hold about people in poverty: they shouldn't have taken such a lousy job, they should have gotten a better education, they're lazy or unreliable or did something that got themselves into their situation. So it is particularly important to frame the minimum wage as good for the entire economy, for *all of us*.

Don't say . . .

- Help the poor
- The working poor

Say . . .

- An economy that works for all of us
- An honest day's pay for an honest day's work

Why . . .

By all means, you can say that "in the wealthiest nation on Earth, no one who works full-time should have to live in poverty." And it would be hard to testify on the minimum wage before a legislative committee without mentioning the federal poverty level. But when you're talking to average voters, avoid referring to beneficiaries in ways that evoke a "welfare" stereotype.

Right wing argument: The free market takes care of wages.

Say . . .

In America, everyone who works hard should be able to live a decent life. Currently, minimum wage workers earn less than $300 a week. No matter where you live, that's just not enough to make ends meet. This is about people who work hard every day so their employer can make a profit. At the very least, they deserve to be able to pay their bills.

Why . . .

An individual who works full-time at the current $7.25/hour federal minimum wage earns $14,500 *a year (for 50 weeks), which is below the poverty level for a family of two or more.* Congress last raised the minimum wage in 2007. The minimum wage in 1968, if adjusted for inflation, would be about $12 today; so raising it to $10-$12 would be modest by historical standards.

Right wing argument: The minimum wage affects only a tiny percentage of workers.

Say . . .

Every hardworking American should get a decent wage. In fact, a minimum wage increase to $10 [or $12, or $15] an hour would improve pay for about one in four private sector workers across the country. And it would benefit everyone else by putting money back into local businesses and getting our economy moving again.

Why . . .

A $10/hour minimum wage would directly boost the wages of about 17 million workers. In addition, because of a "spillover effect"—that increasing everyone below $10/hour would indirectly boost the pay of workers who earn between $10 and $11/hour—the minimum wage increase would benefit 11 million more. Obviously, a minimum wage above $10 an hour would benefit a greater number of Americans.

Right wing argument: Raising the minimum wage will cost jobs.

Say . . .

Every hardworking American should get a decent wage. In fact, a minimum wage increase to $10 [or $12, or $15] an hour would improve pay for about one in four private sector workers across the country. And it would benefit everyone else by putting money back into local businesses and getting our economy moving again.

Right wing argument: Tipped workers are already paid enough. They don't need a raise.

Say . . .

Tipped employees, like waiters, work hard for their pay. And yet, incredibly, the minimum wage for tipped workers is only $2.13 an hour, and it has not increased since 1991. No wonder the poverty rate for tipped workers is more than double the rate for other employees. Raising the tipped minimum wage does not hurt restaurants. In fact, seven states—including California, Minnesota, Nevada and Washington—have the same minimum wage for tipped workers as they have for everyone else, and the restaurants in those states are thriving. Everyone who works hard deserves to make a decent living.

SECTION THREE

HOW TO PRESENT AND REFUTE

HOW TO PRESENT AND REFUTE

18. How to Improve Nonverbal Presentation

You may have the best political ideas in the world (from PLI's *Progressive Agenda*!) and employ the best messaging (from PLI's *Voicing Our Values*!) but still communicate ineffectively because of a failure in non-verbal communication.

In face-to-face communication—whether you are giving a speech, making a fundraising pitch, or talking to neighbors at their doors—*what you say* can be overridden by *how you say it*. That's because your listeners rely on non-verbal information, like body language and verbal tone, to determine what you *really* mean.

A famous study by Albert Mehrabian, Professor Emeritus of Psychology at UCLA, found that an audience interprets a speaker's words:

- from visual clues (facial expression and body language) about 55 percent of the time;
- from tone of voice about 38 percent of the time; and
- from the speaker's actual words only about 7 percent of the time.

Mehrabian's work also demonstrated that when a speaker's words and non-verbal messages are in conflict, the audience consistently defaults to the non-verbal. There are several common situations where this research is important to you.

First, when people are trying to decide whether or not they *like* you, they will pay most attention to your non-verbal expression. Politics is a popularity contest of sorts and whether you win or lose often depends on whether people like you enough to listen.

Second, when people are trying to decide whether they *trust* you, they will again pay most attention to non-verbal cues. For example, if you use strong words about a policy problem but your shoulders are slumped, your hand gestures are weak, and your voice is high, they simply will not trust what you are saying.

Third, when people are trying to decide whether to *believe* what you are telling them—because they aren't familiar with the facts of the matter—they focus on non-verbal "proof" of the matter. This is very important when communicating with persuadable Americans because they pay the least attention to the nuances of politics or policy.

Fourth, if people *disagree* with your position on an issue, they will still use non-verbal cues to make up their minds about you. For example, they may disagree with particular facts or ideas but decide to support your side anyway because you come across, non-verbally, as a stable and trustworthy person.

In short, we all use our emotions to help us decide what to think. Oftentimes we will first form an opinion based on our emotions and then look for facts to support that opinion. When the verbal and non-verbal are in conflict, people trust the non-verbal. So it is essential to make your best possible non-verbal presentation.

About your posture: You don't want to give the appearance of weakness or insecurity. So don't stand with your feet too far apart, or locked side by side. Don't sway forward, slouch, crouch over or put all your weight on one hip. Don't let your arms hang limply at your sides, droop your shoulders or look down. Don't cross your arms, clasp your hands in front of you, put your hands on your waist or in your pockets.

Instead, adopt a posture that projects confidence. Stand up straight, with your feet shoulder width apart, and balance your weight over the balls of your feet. Keep knees and hips in line with the middle of your feet (not forward or back). Relax your shoulders, keep your chest up and stomach in. Hold your head upright and straight with your chin elevated slightly. Hold arms at your sides, in a controlled manner with fingers slightly curled; (this takes a little getting used to, but it is a very open posture to assume). Overall, stay alert, but relaxed.

About your movement and use of space: Don't move just for the sake of moving; don't rock, sway, pace, or race back and forth across the stage. Don't move forward toward the audience too suddenly (aggressively), and don't lean on the podium.

Instead, own your space; give the appearance of control and purpose, in a natural manner. Use gestures as you move, then re-establish good posture when you stop. Scale your gestures to the size of the audience/room. Step forward to establish a connection with an audience member, or to signal you are about to make an important point. Step backward as you conclude an important point, or to create a verbal and physical pause. Move laterally to strengthen a transition between thoughts.

About your gestures: Don't over-gesture. Don't use gestures that don't feel natural to you, in other words, don't try to "play" politician. Don't cross your arms (cold, closed), or clasp your hands in front of you (weak), or put your hands on your waist (too parental), or put your hands in your pockets (nervous). Don't touch your hair, face or neck (nervous), or put your hands behind your back (what are you hiding?), or use gestures that are much wider than your body (out of control), or use too many large gestures (chaotic).

Instead, use gestures that match your presentation. Incorporate natural gestures that you do spontaneously when practicing your remarks. Film yourself if that helps. You can use hands open, palm up at a 45-degree angle, to express honesty and openness; hands open, palms down, to express certainty; and hands open, palms perpendicular, to express measurement or movement. Use gestures that go somewhat wider than your body (for a large concept or idea), but "stay in the frame" even if there's no camera. Be sensitive to cultural differences; use gestures that mean the same thing to the audience as they do to you.

About your facial expressions: You want to avoid looking nervous, harsh or wooden. Don't smile constantly, lick or bite your lips, or tighten your jaw. Don't scowl, sneer or shake your head "no" when you mean "yes" (you'd be surprised how many people do this).

Instead, use facial expressions purposefully. Smile but make sure your expressions match your points. Practice in front of a mirror, especially if you are naturally prone to having a "poker face." Arch your eyebrows to indicate skepticism.

About your eye contact: Don't scan the room generally, or look only at one area of the room, or dart your eyes around the room, or try to look at everyone, or methodically work through the room section to section. Don't look at your notes or slides more than you look at people. Don't bore down on people, or look at the top of people's heads, or just at the back row.

Instead, try to maintain eye contact 90 percent of the time—natural eye contact. Make eye contact with individuals in the room, make a connection with people who are nodding *and* frowning, and connect with people who help humanize your points (i.e. look at a parent with her child when making a point about education). Maintain eye contact with the same person for one complete sentence or thought. In a large room, focus on the sections about two-thirds of the way back from the front. Be sensitive to cultural and gender differences; gently look away if it seems someone is uncomfortable with you looking at them.

About your breathing: Don't forget to breathe, or forget that shallow breathing will make your voice sound more shrill (louder, maybe, but not more powerful).

Instead, practice breathing deep and exhaling slowly. Take a breath before you start speaking, use deep breathing to form a natural, powerful sound, breathe during pauses, and breathe through verbal tics (i.e. "um," "ah").

About your voice: Don't speak in a monotone, or speak too quickly or mumble. Don't use words you can't say, (i.e. avoid "s" words if you have a lisp, and don't use words you routinely stumble over).

Instead, practice an even but slightly varied tone. Employ breathing exercises if your voice is squeaky and high (more common with women). Pause just before and after an important word or concept to allow your audience to absorb that you are making an important point, and speak in an appropriate voice, (i.e. conversational at a house party, authoritatively in a debate).

About your volume: Don't raise and lower your volume too many times (erratic). Don't try to use volume to convey power; a powerful voice comes from proper breathing. And don't speak over applause, laughter, etc.

Instead, project your voice and articulate clearly. Use volume purposefully, make sure you are using it to convey the proper tone. Raise the volume to convey excitement, anger, indignation, energy, and lower your volume to convey seriousness and draw people in. Learn how to use a microphone properly and practice raising your volume if you are soft-spoken and generally hard to hear. Conversely, lower your volume if you are a naturally loud speaker. Minimize noise distractions (i.e., ask for lunch to be served before your speech, and close windows).

About your pitch: Don't keep your pitch high (unless you want to be perceived as weak, nervous and less truthful), and don't vary your pitch too frequently.

Instead, lower your pitch to convey authority and credibility (women naturally have a higher pitch than men, but both genders usually benefit from lowering their pitch somewhat). Relax and take deep breaths, and vary your pitch (higher to convey excitement, lower to convey seriousness). Practice your inflection.

About your tempo: Don't lift the end of your sentences unless you are, in fact, asking a question, and don't lose the audience with long, run-on sentences.

Instead, vary the tempo, or pace, of your speech. Practice speaking 150-160 words per minute (a slow speaker speaks 120/minute and a fast speaker 190; planning 150-160 will allow you to vary your tempo). Use a faster tempo to convey excitement, importance, and a slower pace to convey seriousness. Use appropriate sentence length to match your speaking style and to allow the audience to absorb what you are saying. And use pauses to transition between ideas, call attention to an important thought and capture attention.

All of you public speakers out there, think about how you spend your time when preparing to give a speech. Are you like most policymakers and leaders we've worked with—focusing exclusively or almost exclusively on the *words*? We urge you to thoroughly practice your non-verbal presentation. That's what friends (and mirrors) are for!

19. How to Argue Against Conservative Economics

Conservative philosophy is wrapped up in the language of *free market* economics. To right wingers, freedom means *laissez-faire* policies, opportunity means unregulated markets, and security means defending the rich and their wealth.

The fundamental challenge for progressives is that typical American voters believe in *free markets.* Why shouldn't they? They hear no real arguments to the contrary. But the truth is, there's no such thing as letting the market decide. It's a myth, a fantasy, a fairy tale about a place that does not exist.

American markets are not, and never were, free of government influence. Just open up the business page of any major newspaper and look for yourself. One company seeks to change a law or regulation to its benefit. Another receives a tax abatement from local government. A manufacturer threatens to move overseas unless government provides a subsidy. The Fed increases or decreases the prime rate, affecting everyone's ability to borrow.

We're all familiar with some of the laws and regulations that police markets in order to protect employees, consumers, stockholders, and competing businesses. The government inspects food and drugs, keeps unsafe consumer products off the market, regulates air and water pollution, requires minimum safety and health standards for employees, prevents monopolies, protects consumer privacy, insures bank deposits, and so on.

Voters are less familiar with the many ways that governments warp markets on behalf of the rich and powerful. To name just a few: governments pay direct subsidies (like farm subsidies), indirect subsidies (like loan guarantees), tax abatements (for construction), tax credits (for everything conceivable), and tax loopholes (which allow many big corporations to pay no taxes at all); governments may overpay favored firms or industries for construction, products or service contracts, or allow unconscionable cost overruns; governments set up markets with only a few privileged owners (like the gambling industry); our federal government is one of the most protectionist in the world; and our federal labor laws tilt strongly anti-union (in labor-organizing elections, for example).

In sum, the government is always involved in business, always biasing market results, always nudging and twisting and bumping around the so-called invisible hand. In fact, markets would be more accurately visualized as a multiplicity of hands all engaged in a vast wrist-wrestling contest… with many of them controlled by governments.

If conservative economists actually believed in free markets, wouldn't they be railing against all the pro-corporate market distortions caused by government preferences? But they aren't. That's because they don't really want government to keep its nose out of economic decisions; they want the government to step in and prejudice the market in their favor. They use the term free market not as a philosophy to follow but as a rhetorical device—albeit a hugely effective one—to skew public opinion toward conservative economic policy.

So, Americans are stuck in the wrong debate and it's your job to change that. The question is not whether government should be involved in the marketplace. It is. The question is, what principles should guide government's involvement?

Fair markets

Progressives lack an easily explained, competing economic theory. We need a convincing progressive vision of what makes our economy work, and what would make it work better. What's the first step?

Don't say *free markets* when you're talking about the economy, say *fair markets*.

Don't say . . .	**Say . . .**
• Free markets	• Fair markets

Why . . .

Progressives are for fair markets. By fair, we mean markets that are balanced—with government as a counterweight when necessary—so that weaker individuals and organizations compete on a reasonably equal basis against more powerful ones. In many cases, balancing markets doesn't require more government involvement, it requires less: taking away the subsidies and other unfair advantages that some individuals and businesses enjoy over others.

It is balanced markets that do the most to lower prices, spur innovations, and encourage the kind of hard work that benefits all of society. In contrast, society does not benefit—instead, everyone loses—when people get rich by gaming the system, by exploiting tax or regulatory loopholes, by dismantling viable companies, or by creating scams that aren't technically illegal but should be.

Unbalanced markets weaken competition by giving special advantages to certain companies or specific industries. When a company makes its money through unfair competition, it has little incentive to *build a better mousetrap.* And when a company sells faulty mousetraps to the military at inflated prices, there's even less incentive to change. In fact, the dominant free market ideology gives corporate leaders and their right-wing cheerleaders a strong incentive to corrupt the system. So that's what they've done.

Because Americans accept unfair markets—and in fact, take the unfairness for granted—we don't consider the enormity of the special interest game-playing in Washington. In the current Administration, nearly every economic effort is designed to make markets more unfair. Whether it's tax policy, health care, the federal budget, financial regulation, education policy—or anything else—the proposed policies are designed to tilt the economic playing field even farther toward the rich.

Progressive economist Dean Baker summarizes the situation better than we can:

> The market is just a tool, and in fact a very useful one. It makes no more sense to lash out against markets than to lash out against the wheel. The reality is that conservatives have been quite actively using the power of the government to shape market outcomes in ways that redistribute income upward. However, conservatives have been clever enough to not own up to their role in this process, pretending all along that everything is just the natural working of the market. And, progressives have been foolish enough to go along with this view.

Let us muster a little cleverness of our own. Let's reject the language of free markets and embrace the progressive principle of fair markets.

20. How to Rebut Logical Fallacies

Progressives have gotten so used to hearing bald-faced political lies that perhaps we have become a little less ready to recognize rhetorical tricks. Let us consider five of the most common informal logical fallacies—arguments that may sound convincing but actually rely on a flaw in logic.

(1) Red Herring Fallacy

Also known as: misdirection, smokescreen, clouding the issue, beside the point, and the Chewbacca defense.

A Red Herring argument is one that changes the subject, distracting the audience from the real issue to focus on something else where the speaker feels more comfortable and confident.

EXAMPLE: "It may be true that the minimum wage should be adjusted, but the real solution is to eliminate burdensome government regulations so businesses can grow and be able to pay their employees higher salaries."

Your response should be:

Say . . .

This is not an either-or question. Right now, we're debating specific legislation before the legislature/council to increase the minimum wage to $15 per hour. I'm saying it provides hard-working families with income to spend on their basic needs. Let's talk about that.

(2) Strawman Fallacy

Also known in the U.K. as Aunt Sally.

A Strawman argument is an intentional misrepresentation of an opponent's position. It sets up an easy (and false) target for the speaker to knock down.

EXAMPLE: "The pro-abortion lobbyists oppose a waiting period and sonogram requirement because they favor abortion on demand. And abortion on demand means eliminating all consideration of the unborn child as well as women's health."

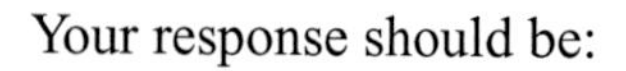

Your response should be:

Say . . .

That is not the issue before this legislature. We are currently debating whether politicians should interfere in a woman's most important and personal life decisions. I'm saying our goal must be to promote people's health and well-being, not impose someone's beliefs on others.

(3) Slippery Slope Fallacy

Also known as absurd extrapolation, thin edge of the wedge, and camel's nose under the tent.

A Slippery Slope argument is a version of a Red Herring. Specifically, this is a claim that a policy which takes a small step in one direction will lead to a chain of events that will result in drastic change.

EXAMPLE: "If we require background checks for the sale of all guns, including private sales at gun shows, it will lead to the federal government obtaining the information to create a list of who owns guns which, in time, will lead to the confiscation of privately-owned firearms."

Your response should be:

Say . . .

We are debating a specific proposal which clearly and obviously does not include your concern. If I argue for driver's licenses are you going to say it will lead to bicycle licenses? If I argue for cleaner drinking water are you going to say it will lead to a shutoff of all water? Let's debate the issue of background checks—why do you think we should sell these guns to any adult whatsoever, no questions asked?

The gun lobby uses Slippery Slope more than anyone. But it's also fairly common in many other areas of debate, e.g., If we allow the sale of marijuana, it will lead to the legalization of all drugs.

(4) Begging the Question Fallacy

Also known as: assuming the initial point, chicken and the egg, and circular reasoning.

In an argument Begging the Question, the conclusion is assumed in one of the argument's premises, and that premise is not supported by independent evidence. Often called circular reasoning, it begins and ends at the same place. [Sorry, it has nothing to do with prompting someone to ask a question.]

EXAMPLE: "Our Second Amendment rights are absolute, so gun control laws are illegal."

Your response should be:

Say . . .
I am arguing for a specific policy and you are responding with a circular argument that's supported by no evidence at all. Background checks for gun purchases have been required by state and federal laws for decades, the only question is whether we're going to apply the law to everyone or continue to have a nonsensical and dangerous loophole.

(5) Post Hoc Fallacy

From the Latin phrase "post hoc, ergo propter hoc," *which means "after this, therefore because of this." Also known as false cause.*

A Post Hoc argument is one where the speaker confuses correlation with causation, specifically, that because one event followed another, the first event caused the second. Is there a so-called Education Reform argument that's not Post Hoc?

EXAMPLE: "Schools that teach Latin have higher test scores, therefore if we establish a school that teaches Latin, it will improve student achievement."

Your response should be:

Say . . .
You are confusing correlation with causation. There is absolutely no proof that teaching Latin causes children to score higher but there is every reason to believe that high-scoring children take Latin. Let us get back to the real point: Our families and our communities need our public schools to provide each and every child the opportunity to achieve their fullest potential in life. There are no standardized children, each one has their own challenges and needs. The question is, how are we going to ensure that?

21. How to Answer Twenty Tough Questions

The following questions are phrased from a relatively hostile point of view. Whether the questioner is actually hostile or just curious, your best answer always starts at a point of agreement and uses values.

1. Do you favor abortion on demand?

Say . . .

Abortion is a complex issue for the individuals involved. It's a decision that's not going to be made any better—medically or morally—by politicians who don't know anything about the circumstances. This very personal and private matter should be decided by individuals, not the government.

Note . . .

The first sentence agrees with the great majority of voters who hold conflicting feelings about the issue. Calling it a *personal and private decision* brings to mind the value of privacy and works in poll after poll. However, keep in mind that most people are not persuadable and anyone who asks the question in such a biased manner is not likely to change positions. Give your best answer and move on. For a longer explanation, see Chapter 13.

2. Should we give special rights to gay people?

Say . . .

If America stands for anything, it's equal opportunity for all. If you have two children or grandchildren, and one is straight and the other gay, you still love them equally. You know the government should treat them fairly and equally. So LGBT people should be treated like everybody else and the law should ensure they're not the victims of discrimination just because of who they are.

Note . . .

The equal opportunity frame usually works best. Appeal to love and finish with the antidiscrimination law that Americans overwhelmingly support. For more discussion, see Chapter 6.

3. Do you favor "opportunity scholarships"?

Say . . .

We all want what's best for our own children. If parents decide private school is best for their child, that's great. But taxpayer dollars should not be taken out of our public schools to fund private schools. We need to focus our scarce tax dollars on the goal of having top-quality public schools so that each and every child has the opportunity to succeed, achieve, and live the American Dream.

Note . . .

The substance works because Americans oppose vouchers if they take money from the public schools. The bottom line: shift the debate away from *failing schools* and toward the importance of providing *opportunity for all*. For more about education, see Chapter 8.

4. Aren't public employees like teachers, firefighters and police getting too many health and pension benefits that taxpayers just can't afford?

Say . . .

Our state/city/county should not waste a penny. We should pay fair wages and benefits, nothing more and nothing less. Based on what I've seen, I do not believe that the teachers, police officers and firefighters in our community are overpaid. But there are some government contractors with excessive subsidies or sweetheart contracts, and we've got to crack down on those to save taxpayer dollars.

Note . . .

Polls show that die-hard conservatives think public employees are overpaid, but persuadable voters generally don't feel that way. Refer to teachers and other public employees *in our community* because voters are much more supportive of public employees they know, especially schoolteachers, than faceless bureaucrats. Then move the discussion to the related issue of overpaid government contractors. This works best if you can show an example of corporations being overpaid in your jurisdiction. It shouldn't be hard to find one.

5. Do you favor gun control?

Say . . .

I support the Second Amendment. But like most Americans, I also support reasonable laws that help keep guns out of the hands of convicted felons, domestic abusers and the dangerously mentally ill. This particular gun violence protection legislation is just a modest, common sense measure to protect our public safety.

Note . . .

Persuadable voters support the Second Amendment. At the same time, 97 percent support requiring background checks for all gun purchases. By all means, appeal to *common sense*. For more about gun legislation, see Chapter 12.

6. Do you favor prayer in schools?

Say . . .

I'm for freedom of religion. Children can freely pray in schools now, if it's voluntary. The problem is government-sanctioned prayer, which was ruled unconstitutional by the U.S. Supreme Court 60 years ago. It violates our freedom of religion for school boards, public schools or teachers to tell children how or when to pray.

Note . . .

People favor prayer in schools. But they also favor upholding our basic constitutional rights.

7. Shouldn't we lock up repeat criminals and throw away the key?

Say . . .

We certainly should lock up repeat *violent* offenders because that makes us safer. At the same time, we are safer if we prevent juveniles and petty criminals from becoming violent career criminals. We can lower the rate of repeat crimes if we send nonviolent drug offenders to addiction treatment instead of putting them in prison. Let's focus on what works to make our communities safer.

Note . . .

Progressives tend to talk about helping criminals. We're right, of course, but that won't work with persuadable voters. Focus on public safety, not the criminal. For more about public safety, see Chapter 12.

8. Do you believe in global warming?

Say . . .

We must protect the health, safety and security of our children and grandchildren. And they face a serious problem. Over 97 percent of climate scientists agree that humans are causing climate change. So we need to apply commonsense strategies now. We know how to implement clean energy solutions and we know that reducing fossil fuel dependence will make America stronger and our kids safer. It's time to step up and get it done...our children are counting on it.

Note . . .

Progressives say *climate change* rather than *global warming*. It polls a little better and it more accurately describes the impact of excessive greenhouse gases. The one key fact that most persuadables don't know is that there is a strong consensus among scientists that climate change is real and humans are causing it. Tie that to the security of your listeners' children and grandchildren. For more about climate change, see Chapter 9.

9. Shouldn't we require drug tests for welfare recipients?

Say . . .

We should certainly discourage people from using illegal drugs. But we need to do it without wasting a lot of taxpayer dollars. States that have tried this policy have found that they spend much more tax money on drug testing than they save in cutting people off from assistance. Drug addiction is a problem across the nation and across income groups. Let's focus on treatment and prevention programs that work.

Note . . .

Polls show that voters support drug testing for public assistance. Right wingers have introduced such legislation in dozens of states. It's a tough issue.

10. Illegal immigrants broke the law. Shouldn't they be deported?

Say . . .

We should be true to American values and protect everyone's right to due process and fair treatment under our Constitution. There are millions of immigrants who work hard and play by the rules, and they make our economy and our country stronger. Further, everyone agrees that it would be logistically impractical and outrageously expensive to seize and deport millions of people. The solution is for Congress to fix the federal immigration process, creating a roadmap to legal residence and citizenship.

Note . . .

Only the far-right base wants to deport all immigrants. Everyone else wants to fix the system.

11. Shouldn't schools teach the controversy between evolution and intelligent design?

Say . . .

The founders of our nation strongly supported freedom of religion. After all, many of their families came here to escape governments that imposed religion upon their citizens. So freedom of religion is the very heart of America. Virtually all scientists agree that intelligent design is not science, it is religion. That's why children should learn about it in church, not in public school science classes.

Note . . .

Intelligent design is a difficult issue because half of Americans believe in some form of creationism, so you've got to lean heavily on their values. Religious people value freedom of religion.

12. Do you favor the death penalty?

Say . . .

Our criminal justice system should be focused on making all of us safer. Since there is not an ounce of evidence that the death penalty deters any crime at all, we shouldn't spend the enormous amounts of time and money needed to implement it. Instead, we should insist that our courts, prosecutors and police divert those resources toward efforts that actually diminish crime. Besides, there are so many people who have been sentenced to death who were later proven innocent. That's an awful injustice, and it also pretty well guarantees that the real murderer remains at large and continues to threaten everyone's safety.

Note . . .

Again, as much as possible, focus on public safety instead of injustice.

13. Do you think that "corporations are people"?

Say . . .

Corporations are not people. They are pieces of paper; they are contracts with the state. Corporations are necessary for doing business and our laws should enable people to run businesses successfully. But corporations don't deserve rights that are fundamental to people, like freedom of speech, freedom of religion, and freedom of assembly. Those rights belong to you and me.

Note . . .

It was Mitt Romney who said, "Corporations are people, my friends." The idea that corporations have the right to freedom of speech is central to the *Citizens United* ruling that has resulted in uncontrolled spending in elections.

14. Doesn't environmental regulation lead to higher energy prices?

Say . . .

None of us likes it when prices rise. But I only support new rules that provide more benefit than cost. Environmental rules protect something that we all own together—our air, water, forests and parks—from abuse by just a few people. When they pollute for profit it is at our joint expense. We need fair and transparent rules to make sure environmental costs aren't dumped on all of us.

Note . . .

Make the environment real to listeners. For more about the environment, see Chapter 9.

15. Shouldn't we stop the construction of a mosque in our neighborhood? They're terrorists!

Say . . .

Freedom of religion is fundamental to America. The key to defending freedom is this: if we deny freedoms to other hardworking law-abiding people, that's how we lose them ourselves. In this case, if a town can block construction just because it's a mosque, then it can block Mormons or Seventh Day Adventists, Methodists or Catholics…or your own denomination. None of us are free unless all of us are free.

Note . . .

People adore freedom but honestly don't understand it. You may have to explain it to them.

16. Wouldn't it hurt small businesses and cost jobs if we increased the minimum wage?

Say . . .

Our economy depends on small businesses. We have to encourage them. But all the evidence shows that increasing the minimum wage puts money in the pockets of people who will spend it almost immediately, which quickly generates business for the local economy. If we do it right, raising the minimum wage is a win-win.

Note . . .

American almost worship small businesses. Embrace them! The fact is, voters overwhelmingly support a substantial raise in the minimum wage, so this is not a difficult sell. To appeal to persuadable voters, focus on how the minimum wage stimulates the economy for everyone rather than how it helps the poor. For more, see Chapter 17.

17. Why are you running for office?

Say . . .

The economy is a mess, people are hurting, and our state/city/county is not doing enough to solve the real problems. I'm running because we can do better. Our system works when everyone gets a fair shot, everyone gives their fair share, and everyone plays by the same rules. My opponent's policies are not fair; they rig the system to benefit the rich over the rest of us. My policies would ensure that everyone who works hard and plays by the rules has the opportunity to live the American Dream.

Note . . .

Everyone who runs for office must be ready to answer this question without hesitation. This is a generic example. If you run for office, personalize this to your campaign and your community, and then memorize it and repeat it every chance you get.

18. Are you a tax-and-spend liberal?

Say . . .

I am a pragmatic and commonsense progressive. I support a balanced budget for our city/county/state. And I support tax fairness. We need to identify and cut tax breaks and loopholes that benefit the wealthy few at the expense of all the rest of us. Our overall goal should be to maintain and improve the quality of life here in [location], not just for ourselves, but for our children and grandchildren.

Note . . .

Don't get defensive. Smack this softball out of the park.

19. Are you trying to knock down the free enterprise system?

Say . . .

No, I favor equal *opportunity* for everyone. That requires a system with rules of the road that make economic competition fair and open and honest. We need to ensure that everybody gets a fair shot, does their fair share, and plays by the same fair rules. Our goal must be to ensure that everyone who works hard and acts responsibly has the opportunity to live the American Dream.

Note . . .

Americans are opposed to economic unfairness. This harsh question gives you the opportunity to lay out your basic progressive economic theme.

20. Are you a Socialist?

Say . . .

I support freedom, opportunity and security for all. We call that a Progressive.

Note . . .

If you're in a crowd, smile. That ideologue just did you a favor.

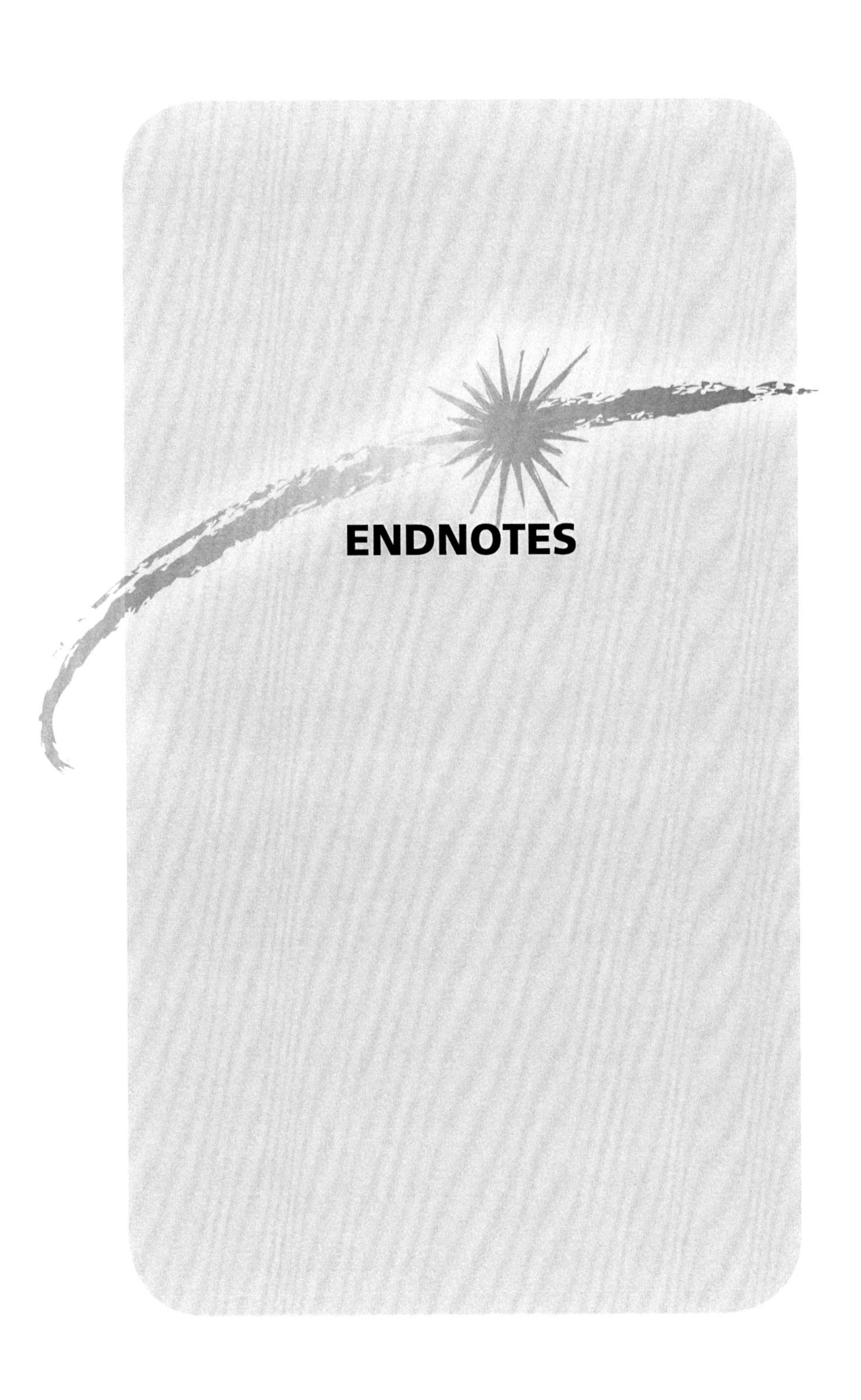

ENDNOTES

ENDNOTES

INTRODUCTION

Page 3 “lies are ubiquitous.” Glenn Kessler, Salvador Rizzo and Meg Kelly, “President Trump has made more than 10,000 false or misleading claims,” *Washington Post,* April 29, 2019.

Page 4 “the majority of Americans who agree with us…” David M. Perry, “The United States is a Progressive Nation with a Democracy Problem,” *The Nation*, February 6, 2019.

SECTION ONE – How to Persuade

1. The Science of Persuasion

Page 7 “the premise that people base their opinions and choices on facts and logical reasoning.” See discussions of the Rational Choice Theory such as Catherine Zuckert, “On the ‘Rationality’ of Rational Choice,” *Political Psychology*, Vol. 16, No. 1 (1995).

Page 7 “In *Thinking Fast and Slow*,” Daniel Kahneman, *Thinking Fast and Slow* (New York: Farrar, Straus and Giroux, 2011).

Page 7 “misconceptions and exaggerations because of biases, heuristics and fallacies.” *See*, for example, David McRaney, *You Are Not So Smart* (New York: Gotham Books, 2011); Chris Mooney, *The Republican Brain: The Science of Why They Deny Science—and Reality,* (Hoboken, NJ: John Wiley & Sons, 2012); Rick Shenkman, Political Animals: How Our Stone-Age Brain Gets in the Way of Smart Politics, (New York: Basic Books, 2016).

Page 7 “Confirmation bias is one of the oldest-known and best-proven cognitive biases.” Raymond S. Nickerson, “Confirmation Bias: A Ubiquitous Phenomenon in Many Guises,” *Review of General Psychology*, 1998, Vol. 2, No. 2, p. 175-220.

Page 7 “Sir Francis Bacon explained it 400 years ago.” Francis Bacon, *Novum Organon*, XLVI (1620).

Page 8 “Friday the 13th is unlucky…” Tom Nichols, *The Death of Expertise: The Campaign Against Established Knowledge and Why it Matters* (New York: Oxford University Press, 2017)

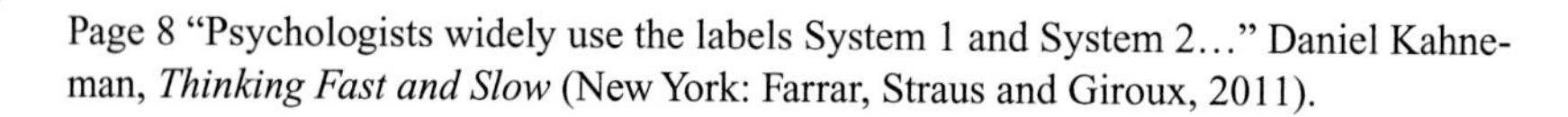

Page 8 "Psychologists widely use the labels System 1 and System 2…" Daniel Kahneman, *Thinking Fast and Slow* (New York: Farrar, Straus and Giroux, 2011).

Page 9 "Clinical psychologist Drew Westen of Emory University… Drew Westen, *The Political Brain: The role in emotion in deciding the fate of the nation* (New York: PublicAffairs, 2007).

Page 9 "As Westen explained in *The Political Brain:*" Drew Westen, *The Political Brain: The role in emotion in deciding the fate of the nation* (New York: PublicAffairs, 2007), p. ix-xv.

2. Three Rules of Persuasion

Page 11 "carry in their minds both progressive and conservative ideas…" *E.g.,* George Lakoff, *Thinking Points: Communicating Our American Values and Vision* (New York: Farrar, Straus and Giroux, 2006), Chapter 2 Biconceptualism.

Page 11 "Persuadables, in contrast, don't pay much attention to public policy…" For much more detail about persuadable voters, their ignorance of political facts and their opinions about values and issues, *see* Bernie Horn, *Framing the Future: How Progressive Values Can Win Elections and Influence Policy* (San Francisco: Berrett-Koehler, 2008), especially chapter 4 "Targeting the Persuadables," p. 47.

Page 12 "Dale Carnegie explained it 80 years ago:" Dale Carnegie, *How to Win Friends and Influence People* (New York: Pocket Books, 1990), originally published in 1937.

Page 14 "Freedom," "opportunity" and "security…" *See* Bernie Horn, *Framing the Future: How Progressive Values Can Win Elections and Influence People* (San Francisco: Barrett-Koehler, 2008). This language is discussed throughout the book and polling about the phrase is reprinted on p. 145-6.

Page 16 "appeals to the *common good*." *E.g.,* Jim Wallis, "Whatever happened to the 'Common Good'"? *Time*, April 4, 2013.

Page 16 "our culture is very, very individualistic." Celinda Lake, presentation of Herndon Alliance research at the FamiliesUSA conference (January 27, 2007).

Page 17 "voters assume that people in poverty failed to help themselves," Pew Research Center/*USA Today*, "Most See Inequality Growing, but Partisans Differ over Solutions," January 23, 2014.

3. Five Mistakes in Persuasion

Page 18 "In his book, *Don't Think of an Elephant*," George Lakoff, *Don't Think of an Elephant: Know your values and frame the debate* (White River Junction, Vermont: Chelsea Green, 2004).

Page 18 "Right wing groups spend millions of dollars on message framing." Peter Stone, "How Newt Gingrich's Language Guru Helped Rebrand the Kochs' Message," *Mother Jones*, December 8, 2014.

Page18 "right wingers want to talk about "border security," asserting that it's an emergency." Brooke Singman and Jake Gibson, "Border arrests skyrocket in May, as officials declare 'full-blown emergency,'" *Fox News*, June 5, 2019.

Page 18 "far below the record pace set during the George W. Bush Administration," Eugene Kiely, "Apprehensions Not 'On Track' to Exceed 1 Million," *FactCheck.Org*, March 8, 2019.

Page 18 "comprehensive reform of the federal immigration system—which Americans agree with," Kent Ingle, "Why are Trump and Congress avoiding comprehensive immigration reform?" *The Hill*, March 10, 2019.

Page 18 "unfair subsidies and tax breaks enjoyed by the rich and powerful—a subject where Americans overwhelmingly side with us." Christopher Ingraham, "Over 60 percent of voters—including half of Republicans—support Elizabeth Warren's wealth tax," *Washington Post*, February 5, 2019.

Page 18 "Climate change…arguments that cannot be effectively denied." Justin McCarthy, "Climate Change Concerns Higher in the Northeast, West U.S.," *Gallup*, April 22, 2019.

Page 19 "stigma attached to the word 'welfare'." Livia Gershon, Why Welfare Reform Didn't End Welfare Stigma, *Daily JSTOR*, August 4, 2016.

Page 20 "saying 'mistakes were made.'" James Fallows, "Mistakes Were Made," *The Atlantic*, February 19, 2015.

Page 20 "Justin Timberlake's agent said," John M. Broder, "Familiar Fallback for Officials: 'Mistakes Were Made,'" *New York Times*, March 14, 2007.

Page 21 "persuadable Americans aren't like us." *See* Bernie Horn, *Framing the Future: How Progressive Values Can Win Elections and Influence People* (San Francisco: Barrett-Koehler, 2008), p. 47-64.

Page 22 "Stories are usually more persuasive than statistics." James Sudakow, "A Good Story Is Always Far More Persuasive Than Facts and Figures," *Inc.*, August 16, 2017.

4. The Politics of Race, Class and Group Identification

Page 23 "Psychology tells us that a great deal of the average person's self-image comes from their social identity." Sarah E. Martiny and Mark Rubin, "Towards a Clearer Understanding of Social Identity Theory's Self-Esteem Hypothesis," *Understanding Peace and Conflict Through Social Identity Theory* (New York: Springer Publishing, 2016), pages 19-32.

Page 24 "Appeals to bigotry cannot be ignored. Polling has found…" Ian Haney Lopez, Anat Shenker-Osorio and Tamara Draut, "Democrats can win by tackling race and class together," *The Guardian*, April 14, 2018.

Page 25 "About 60 percent of Americans are living paycheck-to-paycheck," Josh Boak, "Why aren't many Americans benefiting from the robust U.S. economy?" *Associated Press*, June 15, 2019.

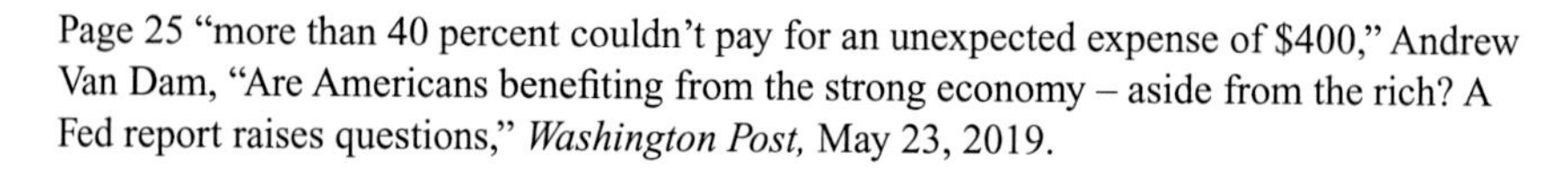

Page 25 "more than 40 percent couldn't pay for an unexpected expense of $400," Andrew Van Dam, "Are Americans benefiting from the strong economy – aside from the rich? A Fed report raises questions," *Washington Post,* May 23, 2019.

Page 25 "on average, credit card holders are carrying negative balances of more than $8,000; and students are leaving college tens of thousands of dollars in debt." Erik Sherman, "New Economic Data Shows Financial Life is Stagnant Or Getting Worse For Many," *Forbes*, September 12, 2018.

Page 25 "the benefits of increased productivity—that is, the creation of wealth within the U.S. economy—were fairly distributed to average workers from the post-war period into the Nixon Administration." Economic Policy Institute, "The top charts of 2016," December 22, 2016, chart 3.

Page 26 "since the end of the Reagan Administration, the richest 10 percent doubled their wealth, while the bottom 90 percent gained just slightly…" Congressional Budget Office, "Trends in Family Wealth, 1989 to 2013," August 2016.

Page 27 "richest one-tenth of one percent of Americans…own about the same amount of private wealth as the bottom 90 percent…" Jon Greenberg, "Warren: Top 1% own about as much as bottom 90 percent," *PolitiFact*, January 31, 2019.

Page 27 "The three wealthiest Americans own more assets than the entire bottom half of the U.S. population." Noah Kirsch, "Members of the Forbes 400 Hold More Wealth Than All U.S. Black Families Combined, Study Finds," *Forbes*, January 14, 2019.

Page 27 "And just 26 people own as much wealth as half of the world's population (that is, 3.8 billion people) combined. Larry Elliott, "World's 26 richest people own as much as poorest 50%, says Oxfam," January 20, 2019.

Page 27 "typical American workers feel that they have been treated unfairly…" Celinda Lake, Daniel Gotoff & Olivia Myszkowski, "Absent a More Progressive Economics, the Democrats Will Lose," *American Prospect*, June 1, 2017.

Page 27 "the economic system…mainly works to benefit those in power." A Washington Post-ABC News poll conducted April 22-25, 2019.

Page 27 "wealthy people have too much power and influence…" An Associated Press-NORC Center for Public Affairs Research poll conducted April 8-11, 2017.

Page 28 "76 percent think 'the wealthiest Americans should pay higher taxes' while only nine percent believe 'upper income people…are paying too much.' and 75 percent think 'corporations should pay higher taxes' while only eight percent believe 'corporations… are paying too much.'" National Tracking Poll by *Morning Consult + Politico*, conducted February 1-2, 2019.

Page 28 "there are already too many special tax loopholes for the wealthiest Americans…" A Global Strategy Group poll conducted April 5-9, 2017.

Page 28 "The third sentence ['everyone gets a fair shot…'] was used by President Obama and polls extremely well." Hart/McInturff, NBC News/*Wall Street Journal* Study #12336 April 13-17, 2012, question 29, where this statement was favored 71-to-28 percent.

Page 29 "Our economy is upside down..." Similar to Greenberg Quinlan Rosner Research for Democracy Corps, October 2011, when the statement was favored by 81%.

Page 29 "A Hart Research poll demonstrated this..." A Hart Research poll conducted for the Center for American Progress Action Fund and published February 4, 2014.

Page 29 "some additional phrases that work:" For more phrases that work, see *Our Story: The Hub for American Narratives* at OurStoryHub.org.

Page 30 "free enterprise has done more to lift people out of poverty..." *see* Hart/McInturff, NBC News/*Wall Street Journal* Study #12336 April 13-17, 2012, question 29, where this statement is favored by 61%.

Page 30 "Americans are in love with small businesses..." Celinda Lake presentation at AFL-CIO, February 17, 2012.

Page 31 "Don't say *capitalism*, *socialism*, or *fascism...*" A Monmouth University Poll conducted April 11-15, 2019.

Page 32 "Conservatives relentlessly warp markets to benefit the rich and powerful." Dean Baker, *The End of Loser Liberalism: Making Markets Progressive* (Washington: Center for Economic and Policy Research, 2011), throughout but especially chapter 1.

Page 32 "American Dream." For public opinion, *see Washington Post*-Miller Center Poll on the American Dream, September 29, 2013.

5. The Philosophy of Progressive Values

Page 33 This chapter is a shortened version of "What We Believe," Bernie Horn, *Framing the Future: How Progressive Values Can Win Elections and Influence Policy* (San Francisco: Berrett-Koehler, 2008), pages 7-22, and the polling is laid out in detail on pages 145-46.

SECTION TWO – How to talk about progressive policies

6. Civil Rights & Liberties

Page 44 "Polls show that there is a tremendous difference in the way Americans feel about unauthorized immigrants..." A CNN/ORC poll conducted March 1-4, 2017.

Page 45 "If you are debating the recent increase at our southern border of asylum seekers..." "Central America Refugee Crisis," USA for the UN Refugee Agency, 2019.

Page 45 "current families at the border are not the same—nor nearly as many—immigrants as those who came by the millions during the Administration of George W. Bush." Jeffrey Passel and D'Vera Cohn, "U.S. Unauthorized Immigrant Total Dips to Lowest Level in a Decade," Pew Research Center, November 27, 2018.

Page 46 "as recently as 2011, a majority of Americans opposed marriage..." A series of Gallup Polls conducted from 1996 through 2016.

Page 46 "Americans support marriage equality by a margin of 2-to-1." A Gallup poll conducted May 1-10, 2018.

Page 46 "Americans support LGBT antidiscrimination laws." A PRRI poll conducted December 2018.

Page 47 "LGBT people have the same values as everyone else." *See* "The LGBT Movement Advancement Project..." The Movement Advancement Project has a series of guides. This section relies most on "Terminology at a Glance: Talking About LGBT People & Equality," "An Ally's Guide to Terminology, Talking About LGBT People & Equality" and "An Ally's Guide to Talking About Marriage for Same-Sex Couples," 2012.

Page 49 "Americans favor posting the Ten Commandments in government buildings by a margin of more than 3-to-1." A Gallup Poll conducted February 25-27, 2005.

7. Consumer Protection

Page 52 "Make it clear that what our right-wing opponents call tort reform isn't reform at all ..." Matters in this section were discussed in Peter D. Hart Research Associates, July 11, 2007, memorandum on civil justice issues.

Page 53 "The Congressional Budget Office reported..." Congressional Budget Office, "Options for reducing the deficit: 2014 to 2023, Limit Medical Malpractice Torts," November 13, 2013.

8. Education

Page 54 "there is too much emphasis on standardized testing in public schools." Rasmussen Poll conducted April 16-17, 2018.

Page 54 "Fifty-five percent oppose linking teacher evaluations to students' standardized test scores. Gallup/PDK Poll, September 2015.

Page 54 "Forty-four percent favor and 35 percent oppose 'the formation of charter schools,'" EducationNext-PEPG Poll, May 2018.

Page 54 "Americans just marginally favor private school vouchers" EducationNext-PEPG Poll, May 2018.

Page 54 "think the focus should be on reforming the existing public school system." PDK Poll, May 1-21 2018.

Page 54 "Americans rate the honesty and ethical standards of teachers as high or very high." A Gallup Poll, "Honesty, Ethics in Professions," conducted December 3-12, 2018.

Page 55 "Sixty-six percent say teachers are underpaid while only six percent think they are overpaid." PDK Poll, May 1-21, 2018.

Page 55 "70 percent would give their school an A or B." PDK Poll, May 1-21 2018.

9. Environment & Smart Growth

Page 58 "about the quality of the environment…" A Gallup Poll conducted March 1-5, 2017.

Page 59 "fracking…" A Gallup Poll conducted March 2-6, 2016 shows that Americans oppose fracking by 51-to-36 percent.

Page 59 Kate Galbraith, "Seeking Disclosure on Fracking," *New York Times*, May 30, 2012.

Page 59 "Since the 2016 election, Americans have been more worried about 'the quality of the environment' than they've ever been in this century," Gallup Poll, March 1-10, 2019.

Page 60 "Polling shows that 65 percent of Americans are 'very' or 'somewhat concerned' about climate change and only six percent believe it 'is not occurring.'" Gallup Poll, March 1-10, 2019.

Page 60 "there is an enormous partisan gap on the issue." Gallup Poll, March 1-10, 2019.

Page 60 "Over 97 percent of climate scientists agree that humans are causing climate change." Abel Gustafson and Matthew Goldberg, "Even Americans highly concerned about climate change dramatically underestimate the scientific consensus," Yale Program on Climate Change Communication, October 18, 2018.

Page 60 "We need to apply commonsense strategies now. We know how to implement clean energy solutions and we know that reducing fossil fuel dependence will make America stronger and our kids safer. It's time to step up and get it done...our children's futures depend on it." This part of the messaging comes from: Breakthrough Strategies & Solutions, "Climate Solutions for a Stronger America: A guide for engaging and winning on climate change & clean energy," August 2012.

Page 60 "The last five years were the hottest year ever recorded for global temperatures…" "The Ten Hottest Global Years on Record," *Climate Central*, February 6, 2019.

Page 61 "Trump voters support taking action to accelerate the development and use of clean energy…" Stephen Lacey quoting Glen Bolger of Public Opinion Strategies in "New Survey Shows That Renewable Energy Polls Extremely Well Among Trump Voters," Greentech Media, December 1, 2016.

10. Government Performance

Page 62 The polling in this chapter comes from two sets of research conducted by Lake Research Partners on July 21-28, 2014 and November 14-22, 2016.

11. Health

Page 65 "As the Affordable Care Act (ACA) has come under attack by the Trump Administration, is has become more and more popular." Kaiser Family Foundation Poll, April 2019.

Page 67 "In fact, 90 percent of Americans believe it is an "important" or "top priority" to pass "legislation to bring down the price of prescription drugs." Kaiser Family Foundation Poll conducted March 8-13, 2018.

Page 68 "smoke-free workplaces:" *See* Campaign for Tobacco-Free Kids, "Voters Across the Country Express Strong Support for Smoke-Free Laws," April 2019.

Page 68 "Americans overwhelmingly believe that secondhand smoke is harmful." A Gallup Poll conducted July 5-9, 2017.

Page 68 "the tobacco tax." *See* Campaign for Tobacco-Free Kids, "Raising Tobacco Taxes: A Win-Win-Win," December 21, 2018.

Page 69 "The American Lung Association…secondhand smoke causes more than 40,000 deaths per year." "Smoking Facts: Health Effects," American Lung Association, 2017.

12. Public Safety

Page 72 "support the 2nd Amendment." Gallup Poll, "Americans in Agreement with Supreme Court on Gun Rights," June 26, 2008, found that 73 percent believe the 2nd Amendment guarantees a personal right to own guns.

Page 72 "more than 10,000 gun murders, 100,000 people shot…" Bureau of Justice Statistics, "Firearm Violence, 1993-2011," (the latest available statistics).

Page 73 "That's why current law requires…" Bureau of Alcohol, Tobacco, Firearms and Explosives, "Brady Law," April 28, 2017.

Page 73 "Poll after poll shows…" Quinnipiac Poll conducted February 16-19, 2018, found that 97 percent of Americans, including 97 percent of Republicans, favor "background checks on all gun buyers."

Page 73 "millions of illegal gun sales…", Bowling, *et al.*, "Background Checks for Firearms Transfers, 2009—Statistical Tables," Bureau of Justice Statistics, October 2010.

Page 74 "*District of Columbia v. Heller*" 554 U.S. 570 (2008).

Page 74 "*U.S. v. Miller*" 307 U.S. 174 (1939).

13. Reproductive Rights

Page 76 "A strong majority of Americans favor keeping abortion legal and oppose overturning *Roe v. Wade*…" An NPR-Marist Poll conducted May 31-June 4, 2019 found 77 percent of Americans support upholding *Roe*.

Page 76 "That research found…" Selzer & Company, Study #2141 for the Public Leadership Institute, conducted August 18-23, 2016.

Page 77 "More than three-quarters of Americans want to uphold *Roe v. Wade*…" NPR-Marist Poll conducted May 31-June 4, 2019.

Page 79 For more answers to right-wing arguments and greater detail on abortion messaging in general, *see* Margaret Conway, "Talking About Abortion," in *A Playbook for Abortion Rights: a guide for state and local policymakers*, (Washington, D.C.: Public Leadership Institute, 2016), p. 1.

14. Social Services

Page 80 "Persuadable voters don't like government on the abstract." D mos, "Issue: What Is Government? And, Can We Talk About Its Role and Purpose More Effectively?" (New York: Dēmos, 2006).

15. Taxation

Page 84 "that upper-income people and corporations are paying too little." National Tracking Poll by *Morning Consult + Politico*, conducted February 1-2, 2019.

Page 84 "Don't say tax relief…" George Lakoff, *Don't think of an elephant*, (White River Junction, VT: Chelsea Green, 2004), p. 3-4.

Page 85 in "Interestingly, a progressive monologue about taxes becomes less popular if it begins with unfairness and then goes on to say what government could do with the money." A Hart Research Associates poll, June 4-10, 2012.

Page 85 "they believe one-third to one-half of tax dollars are wasted." Gallup Poll, "Americans: Uncle Sam Wastes 50 Cents on the Dollar," September 15, 2009.

Page 85 "When all the federal, state and local taxes and fees are added together, almost everybody pays about 20 to 30 percent of their income." Institute for Tax Justice, "Who Pays Taxes in America in 2015," April 9, 2015.

16. Voting & Elections

Page 87 "voter fraud …" See generally, Brennan Center for Justice and Advancement Project, "Debunking the Voter Fraud Myth," January 31, 2017.

Page 88 "many Americans firmly believe that voter fraud exists." A Washington Post/ ABC News poll conducted September 5-8, 2016.

Page 89 "You cannot win the argument by educating voters…" *E.g.*, David C. Wilson, "Public Opinion on Voter ID Laws: Strong Support, Shaky Foundation," July 18, 2012.

Page 89 "*How to Talk About Voting* from the Brennan Center for Justice and the Advancement Project." Brennan Center, "How to Talk About Voting in 2014: A Toolkit for Advocates," 2014.

17. Wages & Benefits

Page 92 "more than 70 percent of Americans favor a substantial increase in the minimum wage," A CBS News/New York Times poll conducted May 28-31, 2015.

Page 93 "would raise it to $15 an hour." Drew DeSilver, "5 facts about the minimum wage," Pew Research Center poll conducted August 9-16, 2016.

Page 94 "persuadable voters will default to negative stereotypes…" Topos Partnership, "Minimum Wage: Presidential Words and Media Reports," February 2013.

Page 94 "below the poverty level…" U.S. Department of Health and Human Services, "2019 Poverty Guidelines."

Page 94 "The minimum wage in 1968, if adjusted for inflation, would be about $12 today;" David Sivak, Fact Check: How Much Would the 1968 Minimum Wage Be Worth Today, Check Your Fact, April 6, 2018.

Page 94 "improve pay for about one in four private sector workers." National Employment Law Project, "Big Business, Corporate Profits, and the Minimum Wage," July 2012.

Page 94 "about 17 million workers." Jared Bernstein and Sharon Parrott, "Proposal to Strengthen Minimum Wage Would Help Low-Wage Workers, With Little Impact on Employment," January 7, 2014.

Page 94 "a minimum wage above $10 an hour would benefit a greater number of Americans." National Employment Law Project, "Fact Sheet: Time to Raise the Minimum Wage," April 23, 2015.

SECTION THREE – How to Present and Rebut

18. How to Improve Nonverbal Presentation

Page 99 "According to Albert Mehrabian…" Albert Mehrabian, *Silent Messages: Implicit communication of emotions and attitude*, (Belmont, California: Wadsworth: 1981).

19. How to Argue Against Conservative Economics

Page 104 This chapter is a shortened version of "Talking About the Economy," Bernie Horn, *Framing the Future: How Progressive Values Can Win Elections and Influence Policy* (San Francisco: Berrett-Koehler, 2008), pages 121-127.

Page 105 "fair markets…" As used here, the term has some similarity to the way it is used in an academic paper by George M. Frankfurter, "The Theory of Fair Markets (TFM) toward a new finance paradigm," *International Review of Financial Analysis 15* (2006) p. 120-144.

Page 106 "Progressive economist Dean Baker summarizes the situation better than we can:" Dean Baker, *The Conservative Nanny State: How the Wealthy Use the Government to Stay Rich and Get Richer*, (Washington, D.C.: Center for Economic and Policy Research, 2006), page v.

20. How to Rebut Logical Fallacies

Page 107 For more discussion of logical fallacies, *see*: Tom Drake, "Drake's List of The Most Common Logical Fallacies," University of Idaho (undated by accessed June 2019).

21. How to Answer Twenty Tough Questions

Page 111 "Americans oppose vouchers…" A PDK/Gallup Poll of the Public's Attitudes Toward the Public Schools, September 2015.

Page 111 "Polls show that die-hard conservatives think public employees are overpaid …" A CBS News/*New York Times* Poll. Feb. 24-27, 2011.

Page 112 "At the same time, 97 percent support requiring background checks…" Quinnipiac Poll conducted February 16-19, 2018.

Page 112 "people favor prayer in schools." A Gallup Poll conducted August 8-11, 2005.

Page 113 "Over 97 percent of climate scientists agree that humans are causing climate change." Abel Gustafson and Matthew Goldberg, "Even Americans highly concerned about climate change dramatically underestimate the scientific consensus," Yale Program on Climate Change Communication, October 18, 2018.

Page 114 "Polls show that voters support drug testing for public assistance …" A Quinnipiac University poll, February 9, 2012.

Page 114 "half of Americans believe in some form of creationism …" A Gallup Poll conducted May 3-6, 2012.

Page 115 "Citizens United…" *Citizens United v. Federal Election Commission,* 448 U.S. 310 (2010).

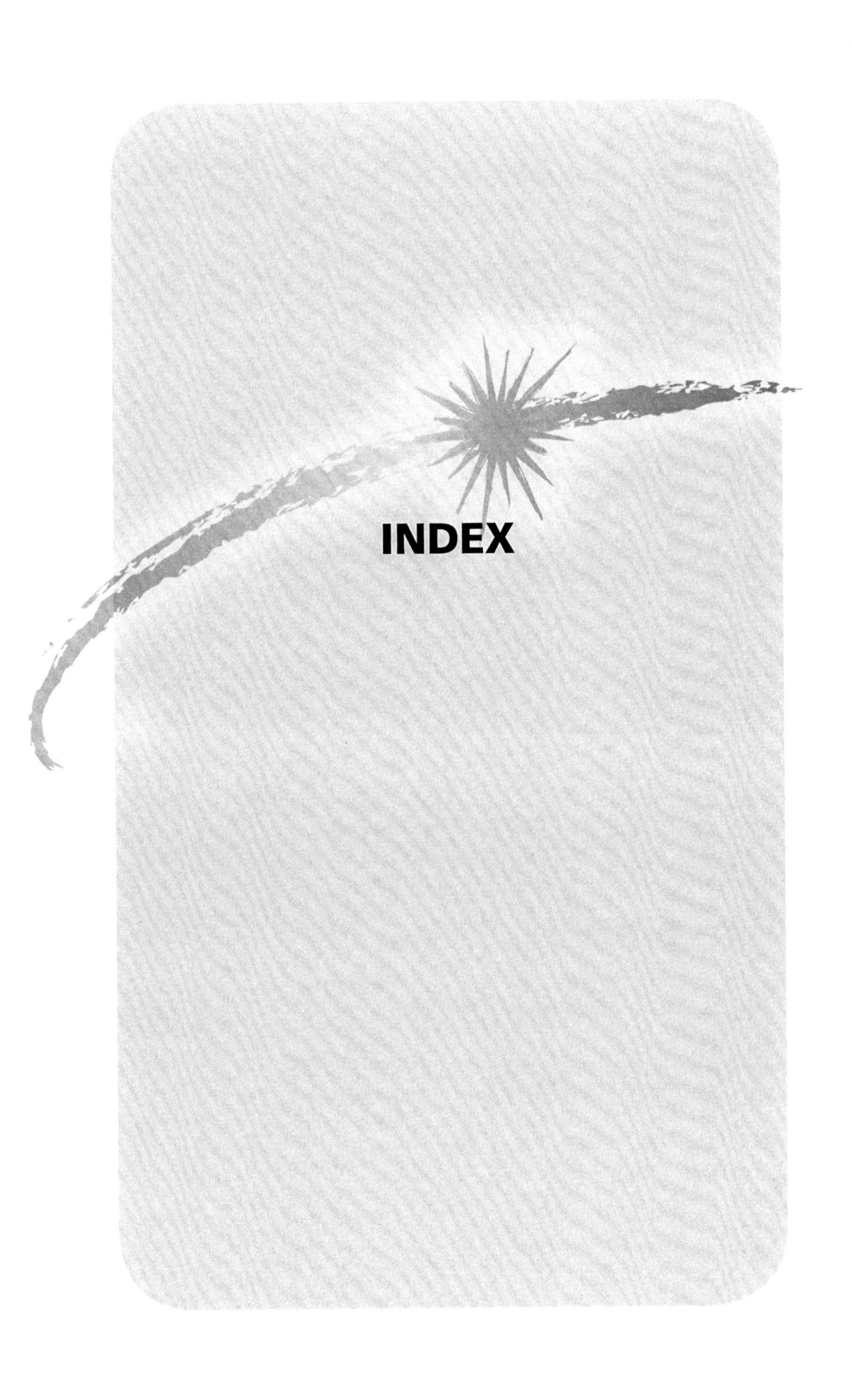

INDEX

INDEX

ACKNOWLEDGMENTS

A large proportion of the messaging advice presented here comes from polls and focus groups conducted by Celinda Lake, who is one of the very best pollsters in America.

Our Story: The Hub for American Narratives (ourstoryhub.org) suggests language for discussing the economy, climate, health care, democracy, immigration, education, criminal justice and more. It's an invaluable resource for progressive messaging.

Some of the messaging recommendations in this book rely on research published or provided by: American Federation of Teachers (education); Americans for Tax Fairness (taxes); America's Voice Education Fund, ASO Communications and The Opportunity Agenda (immigrants); The Bauman Foundation (regulation and enforcement); Breakthrough Strategies & Solutions (climate change); Brennan Center for Justice (voting); Campaign for Tobacco-Free Kids (tobacco); ConwayStrategic (reproductive rights); Dēmos (government); Fair Elections Legal Network (voting); LGBT Movement Advancement Project (LGBTQ); OMP and KNP Communications (gun violence); and Topos Partnership (wages).

ABOUT THE AUTHORS

Bernie Horn is the Senior Director for Policy and Communications at the Public Leadership Institute. He has worked in politics for more than 30 years as a lawyer, lobbyist, political consultant, policy director, and communications trainer.

Bernie is the author of *Framing the Future: How Progressive Values Can Win Elections and Influence People*, published in 2008 by Berrett-Koehler. He was previously a Senior Fellow at the Campaign for America's Future, working on domestic policy and message framing. Between 2000 and 2008, Bernie was Senior Director for Policy and Communications at the Center for Policy Alternatives (CPA). Among other things, he wrote CPA's flagship policy books: eight editions of the *Progressive Agenda for the States* and two editions of the *Progressive Platform for the States*.

From 1994 to 2000, Bernie was President of Strategic Campaign Initiatives, Inc., a political consulting firm that helped elect and reelect hundreds of federal, state and local officials. Additionally, he helped win issue campaigns for increased gun control, tobacco taxes, and health care, and against casino gambling and restrictions on abortion. Between 1988 and 1994, Bernie directed legislative strategy in all state legislatures for Handgun Control, Inc. (now the Brady Campaign), and served as one of the chief lobbyists for the Brady Bill, drafted and lobbied for the federal ban on semiautomatic assault weapons, and conceived the federal ban on handgun sales to minors. Earlier, he was a campaign manager and issues director for congressional campaigns. Bernie is a graduate of the Johns Hopkins University and the Georgetown University Law Center.

Gloria Totten is the President and Founder of the Public Leadership Institute, a nonprofit, nonpartisan policy and leadership center organized to raise public awareness on key issues of equity and justice and to develop public leaders who will improve the economic and social conditions of all Americans.

Gloria has directed nonprofit organizations and led advocacy and electoral campaigns on the federal, state and local levels for 30 years. From 2001-2015, Gloria formed and ran Progressive Majority with the distinct mission to identify, recruit and elect progressive champions at the state and local levels.

Gloria served as Political Director for NARAL from 1996-2001 and Executive Director for Maryland NARAL from 1993-1996. In her home state of Minnesota, Gloria worked on a number of electoral and issue campaigns, as the Education Director for Pro-Choice Resources, President and Lobbyist for the Minnesota Coalition Against Sexual Assault and Media Chair for It's Time Minnesota!, a campaign that expanded anti-discrimination protections to LGBT individuals under the Minnesota Human Rights Code.

Gloria is chair of the board of directors for Brave New Films, a board member for the New American Leaders Initiative and PowerPAC+ and a steering committee member for the Partnership for the Future of Learning. She is an advisory committee member for Oakland Rising Lead East Bay, ProgressNow, re:Power, and the Women's Information Network. Gloria was named a "Rising Star of Politics" by Campaigns & Elections magazine and was awarded the "Progressive Champion Award" by Campaign for America's Future and the "Progressive Leadership Award" by Midwest Academy. Gloria is the co-author of *Voicing Our Values: A Message Guide for Policymakers* and *Preparing to Win: An Advocacy Handbook.*

ABOUT THE PUBLIC LEADERSHIP INSTITUTE

The Public Leadership Institute is a nonprofit, nonpartisan policy and leadership center organized to explore and raise public awareness about key public policy issues of equity and justice and to develop public leaders who will improve the economic and social conditions of all Americans.

PUBLIC POLICY INITIATIVES

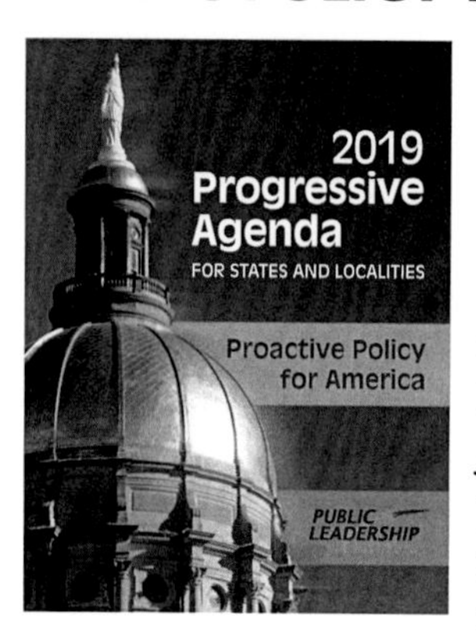

Public Leadership Institute (PLI) creates and disseminates research, talking points and model legislation on a wide range of state and local issues related to economic opportunity, civil rights, education, healthcare, the environment and reproductive freedom. Our best known policy tool is the *Progressive Agenda for States and Localities*, a menu of specific policy ideas and model legislation. Legislators in more than 40 states and council members in more than 50 cities have handed 15,000 copies of the *Progressive Agenda* to their colleagues. PLI also publishes *A Playbook for Abortion Rights* and reports on recent legislation with our *Progress in the States and Localities* and the *Repro Rights Report.* All of our policy resources are accessible through the PLI website.

NATIONWIDE NETWORK

PUBLIC LEADERSHIP INSTITUTE

MODEL LEGISLATION

Pharmaceutical Cost Transparency Act: Last week, Vermont became the first state to enact a Pharmaceutical Cost Transparency Act, requiring drug companies to justify the most egregious Rx price increases. Under the new law, companies must disclose which of the most frequently prescribed drugs have the greatest price increases and the state attorney general is directed to determine the reasons for those increases, ultimately making the information public.

IDEALOG

American Culture is Threatened by Hate Speech: Right now, progressives need to speak out against hate speech and bigotry before it becomes mainstream—the new normal. If we fail to stem the tide of prejudice, our national culture will change and candidates for every office will pander to nativism and white supremacy. Read about it on IdeaLog, our blog intended to raise eyebrows and engage minds.

WEBINAR OF THE WEEK

Get your ideas on the agenda and build support for your policy solutions: Wednesday, June 15 @3pm Eastern, 2pm Central, 1pm Mountain, Noon Pacific. In this interactive session, learn how to build political support to move your ideas forward. This webinar will combine messaging and strategy to get your ideas on the agenda. We will explore no cost and low cost ways to increase awareness of your solutions, activate the public, and build support for your policy ideas. Register here.

RESOURCES YOU CAN USE

Cities and states have been cheating on lead-in-water tests: At least 33 cities and two states have used testing methods that hide dangerous levels of lead in drinking water, according to an investigation by The Guardian. Boston, Philadelphia, Buffalo, Chicago, Columbus and Milwaukee are among the cities that have employed some of the improper testing methods used in Flint,

The Public Leadership Institute hosts the largest network of progressive lawmakers in the nation, with more than 13,000 legislators, council members, commissioners and supervisors, as well as thousands of state-level activists. We communicate with our network every other Thursday through the *PLI Bulletin*, an emailed newsletter that provides hyperlinks directing lawmakers and advocates to the most timely policy news, legislative models, reports, arguments and polls. We also organize networking events, workshops, webinars and conferences, both formal and informal. Whenever appropriate, we link members of our network to policy organizations that can provide special expertise on particular issues.

VOICING OUR VALUES MESSAGE TRAINING

The Public Leadership Institute conducts a program of message and communications training for policy leaders called *Voicing Our Values*. The cornerstone of the program is the annual publication of a message book, also titled *Voicing Our Values*, which includes practical messaging on many specific issue areas (e.g. budget and taxes, education, environment). We have distributed more than 7,000 copies of the book in paperback, it's available on Amazon.com, and it can also be downloaded from our website in PDF format. In addition, we offer bi-weekly message webinars led by policy and communications specialists, and when invited, we present in-state message framing workshops for both elected officials and policy advocates.

LEADERSHIP TRAINING

The Public Leadership Institute conducts policy, communications, media and coalition-building webinars, conferences, trainings, and workshops for policymakers and grassroots leaders. When invited, PLI staff and allied experts present leadership training workshops at meetings across the nation. We hold dozens of training webinars and workshops each year, and every July we present a values-based curriculum at our 3-day conference for state legislators in Washington, D.C.

Public Leadership Institute
1823 Jefferson Place NW
Washington, DC 20036
202-454-6200
www.publicleadershipinstitute.org
leadership@publicleadershipinstitute.org